USA TODAY
A GANNETT COMPANY

HEALTH REPORTS:
DISEASES AND DISORDERS

TOURETTE SYNDROME

MARLENE TARG BRILL

Many people helped me gather information and prepare this book.
I wish to thank Carol Blustein, Tourette Syndrome Association of Illinois; Iris Gimbel,
speech pathologist, for pointing me in the right direction to locate resources and
contact people to interview; and Sue Levi-Pearl, Tourette Syndrome Association,
for her thoughtful reading of the first edition manuscript that was the basis for this
edition. A special thank-you goes to all the caring families who shared their stories,
so others can understand TS better.

Note to readers: The names of people interviewed for this book have been changed to protect their privacy.

Cover image: This micrograph shows neurons in the brain transmitting cellular signals.

Twenty-First Century Books
A division of Lerner Publishing Group, Inc.
241 First Avenue North
Minneapolis, MN 55401 U.S.A.

Website address: www.lernerbooks.com

Library of Congress Cataloging-in-Publication Data

Brill, Marlene Targ.
    Tourette syndrome / by Marlene Targ Brill.
      p. cm. — (USA Today health reports: diseases and disorders)
    Includes bibliographical references and index.
    ISBN 978-0-7613-8144-0 (lib. bdg. : alk. paper)
    1. Tourette syndrome—Popular works. I. Title.
RC375.B752 2012
616.8'3—dc23   2011021411

Manufactured in the United States of America
1 – DP – 12/31/11

CONTENTS

USA TODAY
HEALTH REPORTS:
DISEASES AND DISORDERS

CHAPTER ONE

THE MANY FACES OF TOURETTE SYNDROME

Caroline first noticed her symptoms in second grade. Her head jolted sideways as if she were flicking bangs off her face. Then she began clearing her throat. Her sisters screamed at her to stop the irritating sounds. At first, her parents told her to stop too. But as the sounds continued, her parents worried something awful was happening to their daughter.

Caroline's mother took her to a string of doctors. The first doctor thought Caroline had allergies. He gave her tests and medication—

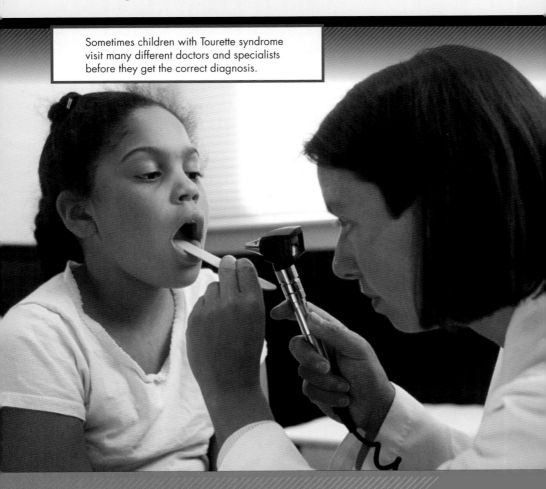

Sometimes children with Tourette syndrome visit many different doctors and specialists before they get the correct diagnosis.

and, later, shots—believing a nasal drip caused the throat clearing. Still, the sounds continued. After several more tests from specialists who never discovered the problem, Caroline's family doctor suggested that she might have Tourette syndrome (also known as Tourette's syndrome or TS). This doctor gave her a different medication, which helped but made her sleepy. When the movements worsened, the doctor upped her dose of medicine, which made her even sleepier. Higher doses created another problem for Caroline: being tired often worsened the unwanted movements. Caroline discovered that controlling her movements with medication required a delicate balance of the right medication and correct dosage.

Unhappy with her daughter's progress, Caroline's mother gave her vitamins, food supplements, and special diets. Nothing prevented the changing parade of symptoms that assaulted Caroline's body. Her jaw twisted until it ached. Her teeth chomped down on the inside of her cheeks, causing the skin to swell. During eighth grade, Caroline produced a series of clicking noises. Most often, they occurred when everyone was quiet, such as during tests. Head jerks and mouth movements, which she found equally embarrassing, were a problem at dances and other social events.

A few classmates made fun of her movements. Caroline never spoke about having TS, but others could see she was having a rough time. "It makes me really mad when my tics become noticeable," Caroline, sixteen, said. "I feel like the odd person, different from everybody."

By high school, many of the painful combinations of twists and jerks faded. Medication still made her sleepy, but it never affected her good grades. Although having Tourette syndrome sometimes left Caroline angry, she came to understand that this was part of who she was. She began telling close friends that she had TS. Little by little, she accepted the movements that were beyond her control.

A PUZZLING DISORDER

Like many people, Caroline had never heard of Tourette syndrome before her doctors and parents explained the disorder to her. Tourette syndrome is a neurological disorder, a disorder of the body's nervous system. People who have TS make movements and sounds, called tics, that are beyond their control.

Thousands of children receive this diagnosis each year. Researchers estimate that TS affects more than two hundred thousand people in

People with Tourette Syndrome

Many well-known and accomplished people have Tourette syndrome, including the following:

- Calvin Peete, professional golfer who won twelve titles in seven seasons

- Dan Aykroyd, comedian, actor, and screenwriter

- Tim Howard, soccer goalkeeper

- Jim Eisenreich, former major-league ballplayer

- Mahmoud Abdul-Rauf, one-time basketball guard with the Denver Nuggets

- Samuel Johnson (1709–1784), author of the first English dictionary, thought to have had TS

- Gary James Marmer, physicist with Argonne National Laboratory and author

the United States alone. About one in one hundred Americans find they have very mild to severe tics, uncontrollable movements that are often signs of TS. For unknown reasons, boys acquire TS three to four times more than girls.

But numbers for all children are increasing. The increase is partly due to better diagnosis but may also be due in part to environmental issues still being studied. Recent reports indicate that three to five people in one hundred may have TS in the United States.

- Mike Higgins, former U.S. Army captain
- Marc Summers, television host and entertainer
- Wolfgang Amadeus Mozart (1756–1791), Austrian composer and pianist, thought to have had TS
- Michael Wolff, jazz pianist, composer, and actor
- Megan Fox, movie actress
- Lowell Handler, photographer and author

Actress Megan Fox is just one well-known person who has Tourette syndrome.

Sports
SECTION C
SPORTS.USATODAY.COM

June 9, 2010

From the Pages of USA TODAY

USA goalkeeper Tim Howard hits his prime at right time

Being a goalkeeper is about anticipation and patience, two contradictory concepts. For Tim Howard, this moment is about both.

On Saturday, Howard, 31, will be the USA's starting goalkeeper when the Americans face England in their World Cup opener in Rustenburg, South Africa. Though heavily favored England has a team full of Premier League stars, the Americans will have a decided advantage at one position: goalkeeper. Howard, who plays for Everton in the Premiership, is one of the world's best.

In 2001, Howard, then with Major League Soccer's MetroStars, became the youngest player to win the league goalkeeper of the year award. But it still wasn't his time. Then-coach Bruce Arena told him the 2002 World Cup would come too quickly for him. Howard was named an alternate.

In 2003, he was plucked from the obscurity of the MetroStars and signed by Manchester United, the world's most famous club. After his first season with United, he was named Premier League goalkeeper of the year. But late in the 2004 season, he misplayed a free kick, costing United a Champions League match, and fell out of favor.

In the 2006 World Cup in Germany, Howard served as backup but didn't play a minute. Before the start of the 2006 World Cup, he verbally agreed to a loan to Everton.

"It was my new lease on life," he says. "The move to Everton was the starting point and the finishing line was in 2010."

When Howard looks back at how he got here, he begins with the stories about the sacrifices made by his mother, Esther. After his parents' divorce, his mother raised [Howard and his brother] in a one-bedroom apartment in North Brunswick, N.J., often working two jobs to cover the travel

Tim Howard dives for a save during a game in 2011 between the United States and Spain. Howard hasn't let having Tourette syndrome get in the way of a successful soccer career.

costs for all of his youth tournaments.

In fifth grade, Howard was diagnosed with Tourette's syndrome. This only increased his focus.

He's a spokesman for Tourette's awareness, serving as an inspiration for children with the same problem.

"T.S. is part of my life. It's like breathing to me," Howard says. "I don't feel that I missed out on anything, and I still don't take medication for it."

The condition increases with anxiety, and since standing in goal as foes fire rockets is stress-provoking, Howard learned how to subdue both. In games, he says, his concentration is so intense, Tourette's doesn't affect his play.

—*Kelly Whiteside*

Some believe that almost 25 percent of school-aged children display tics. Many people struggle through life, feeling something is wrong with them but never have TS diagnosed. Those around them wonder whether their jumpy friends and neighbors are safe to be near.

Part of the TS puzzle is the broad range of symptoms, from barely noticeable to severe and life-altering. Some symptoms appear as occasional jerks or grimaces. Others involve uncontrollable spasms and shouts that can be disabling. Because of such unexpected and uncommon behaviors, a person with TS is often teased or feared. School becomes an endless battle for many children with TS because

Many students who have Tourette syndrome feel isolated from their classmates because of symptoms they can't control.

they refuse to tell anyone, or if they do, classmates are unable to understand their condition.

One way to build understanding, combat prejudice, and open factual discussions about Tourette syndrome is to learn more about the disorder. Perhaps you know someone like Caroline. Maybe you are like some of the other people you will meet later in this book, or you have recently seen a character with TS on television or in a movie. This book is for anyone who wants to better understand this disorder.

CHAPTER TWO

WHAT IS TOURETTE SYNDROME?

Brian's mother first noticed her son's behavior when he was eight weeks old. She saw rhythmic patterns in her baby's arm and leg movements. Within a short time, Brian's wild movements included blinking, and he made low-pitched droning sounds.

By the age of four, he showed promise of being unusually bright. He held conversations like a much older child. Sometimes he could sit and read books for hours. But other times, he turned into a bundle of uncontrollable activity. His flailing legs narrowly missed knocking over furniture, and he rolled his head side to side on the rough carpet, rubbing a bald spot on the back of his head.

One day Brian started jumping rhythmically. After his mother scolded him several times to stop, he said, "I heard you, but my brain is telling me to jump and hum, and it talks louder than you do."

Brian's mother knew something was wrong. Yet doctors told her she was too anxious. They said she had the problem, not her son. To make matters worse, Brian's movements came and went. By the time she arranged a doctor's appointment, any signs of a problem disappeared. Without seeing the movements first-hand, doctors couldn't figure out what caused Brian's actions.

In school, Brian continued to be a study in contrasts. He read Pippi Longstocking at the age of six and Stephen King books by the age of eight. He imitated voices and memorized the entire musical score of Cats, but he could not remember multiplication tables. He was a good athlete, yet hand tremors turned his writing into unreadable chicken scratchings, and he struggled to hit the correct computer keys. Brian was nine when his mother stumbled upon an article that best described him. It was about Tourette syndrome. Armed with this new evidence, she found a doctor who confirmed her diagnosis.

Luckily, Brian always had friends. His keen sense of humor, funny voices, and acting talent attracted other kids. However, he also had a temper. He projected an attitude of "If you tease me, I'm going to punch your lights out."

At home, Brian's temper developed into a major problem. From the age of twelve to seventeen, he never went a day without expressing anger at someone. Situations that seemed unimportant to others caused violent outbursts in Brian. On several occasions, he smashed through the closed glass storm door. For years, his brother feared being alone with him. Brian hated how quick he was to anger and felt sorry after his temper flared. He became convinced he was evil.

Medication and time helped tame the storm inside Brian. He completed high school, but he had trouble holding a job and finishing the college acting classes he loved. He once left a job because his trembling hands couldn't open the lock on his locker. Rather than tell his boss, he quit. Another problem was the panic attacks that began to accompany his TS. He never panicked onstage, but groundless fears kept him from entering the school building or classroom. Still, at the age of twenty-four, Brian refused to give up. He enjoyed writing at home where he felt safe with his mother typing his work. He hoped to one day return to college, perhaps to become a professional author, actor, or director.

TICS

Tics can make everyday life extremely challenging for people with TS. When a tic occurs, the brain tells one or more muscles to contract, causing unwanted sounds or movements. These movements seem to happen without a particular purpose. They come on suddenly and quickly and repeat without warning.

Tics may affect any part of the body at any time. Vocal tics originate in the muscles that control speech. Sounds produced may range from smacking, hissing, and throat clearing to shouts of words or phrases. Motor tics can occur in any muscles of the body, producing various movements from blinking and nose wrinkling to leg jerks, hops, and arm thrusts.

Symptoms and their severity differ widely among people. Tics can be mild, severe, or somewhere in the middle. Not all people with TS exhibit all symptoms. How much TS affects specific behaviors depends on each person's physical makeup. Tics can occur several times a minute or only a few times a day or week. Certain tics

Common Motor Tics

simple:

eye blinking

leg jerking

head jerking

neck twisting

finger moving

tongue thrusting

shoulder shrugging

muscle tensing

nose wrinkling

toe bending

complex:

forming unusual faces

touching other people or things

leaping

twirling

biting, hitting, rubbing, or other self-destructive actions

smelling objects

imitating others' actions (echopraxia)

making offensive gestures (copropraxia)

may remain in some form throughout a lifetime. They may appear elsewhere in the body or change into milder or more severe forms. Some tics, such as temper outbursts, may fade completely with time.

SIMPLE AND COMPLEX TICS

Doctors define tics as simple or complex, depending on the number of involved body parts and muscle groups. Individual movements of only one body part, such as shoulder shrugging or head jerking, are called simple tics. Similarly, individual sounds, such as sniffing

Common Vocal Tics

simple:

sniffing

grunting

throat clearing

lip smacking

belching

hissing

tongue clicking

coughing

yelping

barking

complex:

saying words or phrases out of context

producing animal sounds

repeating a sound, a word, or a phrase someone else just said (echolalia)

repeating one's own words or sounds (palilalia)

saying offensive words or phrases (coprolalia)

spitting

stuttering

and grunting that are produced by forcing air through the nose, the throat, or vocal cords, are simple vocal tics.

Complex tics involve several muscle groups that trigger patterns of movements. Examples of complex motor tics are picking scabs or jumping. More embarrassing tics involve other people, such as touching someone else, imitating others' actions (echopraxia), and making offensive gestures (copropraxia).

Complex vocal tics include echolalia, palilalia, and coprolalia. With echolalia, a person repeats the last sound, word, or phrase said by someone else. For example, after a father says, "Clean your room," his son may repeat, "Clean your room." With palilalia, the boy may repeat his own words or sounds, saying, "I'll clean my room, room, room" or "I'll clean my room-m-m-m."

The most well-known symptom of TS is coprolalia—cursing or saying socially inappropriate words or phrases. When television shows and movies feature a character with TS, they often show that person letting out a string of swear words or sexual terms for no apparent reason. Therefore, many people assume that everyone with TS swears uncontrollably, which is untrue. Less than 15 percent of individuals with TS struggle with coprolalia.

One mother found this knowledge comforting. She didn't understand that many more people have mild TS than severe. When her son was first diagnosed, she panicked. Then her doctor explained that TS has a range of symptoms. She felt relieved to learn what a small percentage of cases involve swearing.

SUPPRESSING TICS

Most children with TS begin ticcing between three and ten years of age. Often the first signs are eye blinking or throat clearing, although any kind of tic can develop. Other tics may soon follow. Without proper diagnosis, children who tic are unsure what is

Tic Triggers

- excitement
- stress
- anger
- fear
- depression
- tiredness
- talking about tics

- infection
- change of routine
- transitions
- new situations
- caffeine or other stimulants

happening to their seemingly out-of-control body.

By early adolescence (between nine and thirteen years), tics may worsen. One cause is the normal surge of hormones that occur at this time. Another cause stems from concerns many teenagers have about their maturing bodies and what others think about them. This added worry and stress only increases symptoms of TS.

The concern about body image has its upside. Like other teens, those with TS gain greater awareness of their body as they mature. The awareness allows them to feel the sudden urge to tic a split second before it happens. With this information, many teens learn to identify what triggers their tics and how to handle them better. Although tics may never fully go away, people can gain some control over when and where they happen.

Many, but not all, who have TS say they can suppress their tics. Some claim to hold back tics for up to thirty minutes or an hour. This allows them time to find a private place to let out the tics. Like

USA TODAY

Sports
SECTION C

SPORTS.USATODAY.COM

February 17, 2006

From the Pages of USA TODAY

Bernotas finds calling on a sled; Focused training helps him cope with depression

As he was battling back from alcoholism and depression, Eric Bernotas used to strap a tire to his waist and sprint uphill in an intense training regimen. The only thing he was lacking was a sport.

Today he is one of the inspirational stories on the U.S. Olympic team and considered the USA's best hope for a medal in the two-heat men's skeleton race [a fast sledding sport].

The 34-year-old Pennsylvanian, who finished third in the World Cup rankings this year, has Tourette's syndrome, still fights depression and turned his life around after—as he puts it—"self-medicating with alcohol" his first few years in college.

He suffers from a mild case of Tourette's syndrome, but he says it doesn't hamper his performance in a sport in which the smallest movement can have a significant effect.

"It doesn't seem to manifest itself when I'm on the sled," he says. "I think the level of concentration is so high and I'm so focused."

Focus was clearly lacking in his troubled period. After an active athletic career at Malvern Prep outside Philadelphia, he drifted aimlessly his first three years at West Virginia University.

Early in his fifth year in college, he was doing side work for a professor and constantly missing deadlines. The conversations, he says, turned from the projects to his problems, and the professor steered him to university counseling, where his depression was diagnosed. The Tourette's syndrome was clinically diagnosed a short time later.

After graduating, he continued the rigorous training more to establish a direction

a sneeze or a hiccup, tics need to be expressed eventually. Trying to hold them in only creates tension inside the body that must be released. Often, delayed tics explode with greater force and last longer than an unsuppressed tic would.

Eric Bernotas competes in the 2010 Winter Olympics in Vancouver, British Columbia. Bernotas has a mild case of Tourette syndrome.

than reach a destination, he says. At the same time, he was hoping to find a sport to pursue. Then came the wrong turn that led him to Torino.

He and a girlfriend missed a highway exit on a trip to Vermont and found themselves near Lake Placid [in New York]. She wanted to see it all; he tagged along and at her urging met with a skeleton coach. One month before the Salt Lake City Games, he was invited back to Lake Placid for a skeleton camp.

He rose quickly in the sport, making the World Cup team in his third season (2004-05), hitting the podium twice, including a gold medal in the final race of the year in Lake Placid.

Bernotas says he's willing to share his story and hopes it somehow helps others.
—*Mike Dodd*

One boy with TS likens the surge of tics to a ball of energy that builds, like having to go to the bathroom. Eventually, the massive amount of energy has to come out. That's when he tries to find a private place to let a couple tics loose. The release produces a sense of relief.

REDUCING TICS

Certain types of activity can reduce tics temporarily. For many people, rhythmic physical activity—exercise—seems to refocus the energy needed to produce tics. Similarly, tics may disappear while the person concentrates on an absorbing activity, such as listening to music, reading, or drawing.

Oliver Sacks, a famous neurologist (doctor who specializes in the nervous system) and author, saw firsthand how focusing eases tics. He followed a surgeon with TS through his daily routine to understand how he could perform such delicate work. The doctor told Sacks that at home he sometimes flung objects—an iron, a rolling pin, saucepans— as if enraged and had compulsions to do everything in threes or fives. At the hospital, Sacks watched in amazement as the doctor walked down hallways skipping at each fifth step. Suddenly, the doctor would reach for the ground as if he were scooping up something.

Dr. Oliver Sacks, a neurologist and author, has studied patients with Tourette syndrome to see how they deal with tics.

In meetings, he tapped coworkers and occasionally rolled on his side to touch their shoulders with his toes. What fascinated Sacks most, however, was the doctor's ability to handle surgery despite all this darting and touching. "B. took the knife, made a bold, clear incision—there was no hint of any ticcing or distraction," Sacks wrote.

DIAGNOSING TOURETTE SYNDROME

Not everyone who tics has Tourette syndrome. Diseases of the nervous system and long-term use of certain mind-altering drugs can cause tics but not TS. A blow to the head, such as from a car accident or in military battle, can injure the brain and leave someone with tics.

Tics normally appear and disappear by themselves in childhood as the nervous system develops. One in five children experiences some kind of tic for a few months or a year during childhood, especially when nervous or under stress. These tics are usually mild and hardly noticeable. Even tics that are visible rarely interfere with everyday activities enough to cause concern.

As yet, no medical tests exist to confirm a TS diagnosis. Instead, physicians diagnose TS after observing symptoms and ruling out other health conditions with blood tests and body scans. They take a careful case history from the patient and parents, who describe their child's behavior and family history. If no other problems surface, doctors follow diagnostic guidelines for TS set by the American Psychiatric Association. According to these guidelines, physicians look for:

- multiple motor tics and at least one vocal tic
- tics that occur several times a day, nearly every day or intermittently, and that last a year without a tic-free period of more than three straight months

- tics begin before the age of eighteen
- tics that aren't caused by medications, other substances, or another medical condition

Even with these guidelines, making a diagnosis can be tricky. The exact cause of TS remains unclear. That is why TS is called a syndrome rather than a disease. A disease, such as the measles or the chicken pox, has known causes and definite signs that signal what it is. With a syndrome, however, there are no blood tests or body scans to prove it exists. A syndrome is a collection of observed symptoms that have been given a name. Therefore, a diagnosis of TS results from observing and reporting.

"My first symptoms appeared at age six," Mark, aged thirty-seven, remembers. "I bit my lip. My parents thought I had a speech problem, so they sent me to a speech pathologist." She couldn't find anything that would cause Mark's symptoms. She suggested sending him to a psychologist. Then barking and other noises and movements started. "Five years later, I got diagnosed only because my parents read about someone [with similar symptoms] in the paper and tracked down the doctor who had diagnosed the person."

Years ago, families went from doctor to doctor because so few recognized the symptoms of TS. Searching for a diagnosis for five to ten years was common. These days, doctors are better able to recognize signs of TS. Still, some diagnoses can take six months to a year after consulting with a doctor about a patient's symptoms. The media, too, are beginning to show the milder side of TS, thereby increasing awareness and acceptance of people with TS. With more positive and accurate information available, people who cope with tics are seeking diagnosis and treatment sooner.

OVERLAPPING DISORDERS

Diagnosis becomes complicated when symptoms of TS appear in combination with other conditions. A wide spectrum of behaviors overlaps or mimics other disorders, some more disabling than TS. Not all people with a TS diagnosis struggle with other disorders. Yet those with TS have a greater likelihood of also having something else.

Many of these disorders share common symptoms. In fact, researchers suspect that several conditions may stem from related causes. Tics may be the most visible sign for people with TS. But their condition may also include obsessive, compulsive, hyperactive, or impulsive behavior. People with these conditions may be disorganized, depressed, or unable to focus. And they may experience sleep, mood, and learning problems.

OBSESSIVE-COMPULSIVE DISORDER (OCD)

Between 25 and 50 percent of children who tic exhibit obsessions and compulsions. Obsessions are thoughts or images that return over and over again. On the simplest level, a person with an obsession can be compared to a child who is stuck on the same bedtime story. In the worst case, obsessions interfere with daily functions so often that they leave the person feeling upset and out of control. For example, some people worry that dirt and germs will infect their body, or they fear harm will come to them or family members. Everything they do revolves around keeping safe and free of disease. People with uncommon worries may also be consumed with thoughts about certain words, objects, or numbers, or they may need things arranged a certain way. Worries and superstitions are part of everyday life. But for someone who is truly obsessed, uncomfortable feelings bring extreme fear, sickness, or doubt.

A few people complain that their mind races with obsessive thoughts, interfering with sleep, speech, and daily activities. One mother remembers: "My son had many thoughts racing through his mind, so he had trouble expressing himself. The thoughts were not always related to what we were talking about at the time or what he wanted to say, so we were always trying to connect why he was saying something. Part of his frustration was we couldn't understand what he was saying."

Compulsions are what obsessive people do to make their discomfort go away. Compulsions are actions that must be performed repeatedly, according to rules defined by the particular obsession. For example, someone who fears germs may wash their hands until the skin cracks. Someone else may touch a specific doorknob a certain number of times to keep strangers away. Similarly, a child may feel an overpowering need to hear a song or to wear a certain pair of socks, or a student may recheck homework so many times that the deadline for handing it in passes.

Washing hands repeatedly because of a fear of germs can be one form of obsessive-compulsive behavior.

Common Obsessions and Compulsions

Obsessions

- suffers unusual worry or doubt
- worries about dirt and germs
- needs order and symmetry
- fears scary or harmful things will happen
- imagines losing control and becoming aggressive
- sees sexual images frequently
- is consumed by moral/ religious thoughts
- mentally rearranges letters and words
- fixated on a number or a letter

Compulsions

- checks and rechecks continually
- practices washing and cleaning rules
- counts things or tries to even up sides or numbers of things
- touches self, others, or objects
- moves or arranges objects by certain number patterns
- arranges and lines up items constantly
- seeks continual approval
- repeats actions
- erases mistakes
- repeats a phrase or a prayer excessively
- hoards and saves things of little or no value

People with obsessions understand that these actions make no sense. But they are unable to control the urge to satisfy them. It's as if their brain gets stuck on a particular thought or urge that prevents them from doing anything else. When obsessions and compulsions become this strong, someone is considered to have obsessive-compulsive disorder. People with OCD often say the symptoms make them feel as if their mind is disconnected from their out-of-control body.

"Obsession is thinking about something, and a compulsion is doing something," explains Mark, who has OCD traits and TS. "You keep doing it until you get it right. It's like a tic, but when I'm ticcing, I don't even know I'm doing it. With a compulsion, there might be a thought process, like when I frequently touch my nose. I keep thinking about the word 'touch.' The compulsion is I got to do it, I got to do it, I got to do it."

ATTENTION DEFICIT HYPERACTIVITY DISORDER (ADHD)

Other common conditions that can occur with TS include attention deficit hyperactivity disorder. The Tourette Syndrome Association reports that between 30 and 40 percent of students with TS also exhibit signs of ADHD. Children who have ADHD find it difficult to focus attention, control impulses, and behave as expected. They are easily distracted by the slightest sound or movement. They have problems concentrating on

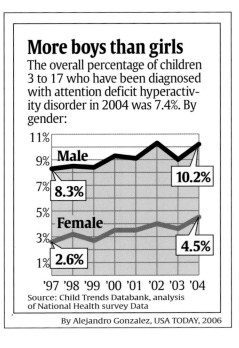

More boys than girls

The overall percentage of children 3 to 17 who have been diagnosed with attention deficit hyperactivity disorder in 2004 was 7.4%. By gender:

Male 8.3% ... 10.2%

Female 2.6% ... 4.5%

'97 '98 '99 '00 '01 '02 '03 '04

Source: Child Trends Databank, analysis of National Health survey Data

By Alejandro Gonzalez, USA TODAY, 2006

what they do and what others say. They lose track of what is going on, leading to endless disorganization. Consequently, they often seem forgetful, unable to follow directions, and incapable of completing schoolwork, chores, or projects.

Children with ADHD often fidget constantly and talk excessively—blurting out answers before questions are completed and interrupting conversations. Usually, children show these signs of being hyper before TS symptoms emerge. In fact, some doctors caution that a few medicines for ADHD bring out or worsen tics for people with TS.

Because they cannot focus well, children with ADHD struggle with relationships. They cannot wait their turn, and they appear never to listen, which drives away friends. In addition, children with ADHD tend to take more risks, possibly because they lack focus to weigh the consequences.

As with TS, symptoms of OCD and ADHD can come and go, so others figure that these behaviors can be controlled. Other people

Students with attention deficit hyperactivity disorder often lose track of what is going on and have problems concentrating.

cannot see the inner thought processes that influence why and how someone who has ADHD or OCD behaves. All three conditions involve problems with the nervous system that are beyond someone's control.

Fourteen-year-old Aaron dealt with multiple conditions. He described his experience this way: "I can be really hyper and out of control. I run around making noises—actually sensations that my chest screams. I used to buy things compulsively. I have more energy than most people, which is a good thing about being hyperactive, and I don't tire easily." Aaron found he could stay up all night watching TV. He had a hard time getting up in the morning but still was too hyper at school. "I get sent to the principal's office a couple of times a day. I have to say over and over, 'I will follow directions and respect people's property.'"

LEARNING DISABILITIES

Tourette syndrome does nothing to change intelligence. But children diagnosed with TS may struggle with schoolwork more than others. Eye blinking, body jerking, or poor impulse control can interfere with learning by making reading, concentrating, and writing difficult.

About 20 to 30 percent of children with TS have serious learning disabilities in addition to tics. The clearest signs of learning disabilities are inconsistent grades and poor performance in at least one area. Usually, these problems stem from difficulty learning basic skills in reading, spelling, writing, and math. Students with a learning disability have trouble processing or acting on information they see, hear, or remember. They try just as hard as other students. But they may fail tests and get bad grades. Unable to cope with their schoolwork, many become frustrated.

"I'm not a good student," Jake, aged thirteen, admits. "I hate to study.

I hate doing homework. Teachers annoy me. I hate school." Without getting help in school, frustrated students with TS often develop this negative attitude. Eventually, they may simply lose interest and stop trying.

SLEEP DISORDERS

Sleep problems are common among people with TS. Sometimes, tics make falling asleep difficult. Once asleep, people who tic may awaken frequently during the night or walk and talk in their sleep. Sleep studies confirm that some people with TS exhibit motor and vocal tics while asleep that are

Learning disabilities can make schoolwork especially challenging for some children with TS.

similar to those observed when awake. Others find that their tics lessen or disappear during sleep.

In Jake's case, his most significant problem in third grade was related to sleep. He went for long periods when his father heard him ticcing in bed. Often he banged his action figures together under the covers to mask his vocal tics. Several years later, even as a teen, Jake still struggled with getting to sleep.

Outbursts of rage can occur in children diagnosed with TS. This is generally difficult to live with, both for the child with TS and for his or her siblings.

CONDUCT PROBLEMS

For unknown reasons, about 30 to 40 percent of those with TS display huge mood swings. Usually, these people also deal with another condition, such as ADHD or OCD. For some with overlapping conditions, extreme feelings overwhelm them on a daily, monthly, or yearly basis. Their outbursts of rage far exceed common temper tantrums and normal personality differences among individuals. The outbursts seem to come from nowhere, with little prompting, and explode into wild fury. Once started, rages must follow their course until all energy is gone. One person with TS claims he has a need to see or feel things break or his rage isn't satisfied. These outbursts are not about anger. They are more about having an abnormally short fuse and an urgent need to let off steam. Afterward, most people who rage feel ashamed or guilty about what they have done.

"I knew very well how awful it felt to be stuck in a rage that there was no excuse for," Brian explains. "The horrible part was that I could not get out of it or even indicate in any way [to my targets] that I knew I was being unfair. I could only wait for it to pass. It was as if a cloud of rage had floated by and seized me, filling me up for a while before it drifted off on its way again."

Finding out that rage was part of his overall symptoms provided great relief to Brian. For years, he had agonized over thinking he was just born aggressive and dangerous. Learning the reason he overreacted helped him come to terms with his condition and deal with the anger.

CHAPTER THREE

WHAT CAUSES TOURETTE SYNDROME?

In 1825 French physician Jean-Marc Itard described troubling behaviors in his patient, the Marquise de Dampierre. Itard had been observing the French noblewoman for nineteen years, ever since unusual motor tics first appeared at the age of seven. Soon she added vocal tics that eventually developed into swearing and screams. He wrote in his notes:

> Madame de D...at the age of seven was afflicted by convulsive movements of the hand and arms. After each spasm, the movements of the hand became more regular and better controlled until a convulsive movement would again interrupt her work....As the disease progressed, and the spasms spread to involve her voice and speech, the young lady made strange screams and said words that made no sense. However, during all this, she was clearly alert, and showed no signs of delirium [being confused] or other mental problems....
>
> In the midst of an interesting conversation, all of a sudden, without being able to prevent it, she interrupts what she

French doctor Jean-Marc Itard documented the behavior of his patient, Marquise de Dampierre, who suffered from what was likely Tourette syndrome.

is saying or what she is listening to with horrible screams and with words that are even more extraordinary than her screams. All of this contrasts...with her distinguished manners and background. These words are, for the most part, offensive curse words and obscene sayings. These are no less embarrassing for her than for those who have to listen, the expressions being so crude that an unfavorable opinion of the woman is almost inevitable.

Although the marquise married, she spent much of her time hidden from polite society. She remained the topic of gossip until her death in 1884 at the age of eighty-six.

LONG HISTORY OF TOURETTE SYNDROME

Tourette syndrome is not new. Ancient Greeks recorded examples of sudden facial movements, barking, and cursing almost two thousand years ago. Since then, physicians from every era have written about individuals who mysteriously twitched and shouted.

Hundreds of years ago, some people with tics were worshipped or thought to be enchanted. Many more, however, were considered mentally ill or were tortured, jailed, or burned as witches. One researcher claimed that several women burned during the 1692 Salem witchcraft trials may have displayed signs of Tourette syndrome. Their tics confirmed to the townspeople that the women were bewitched. Times—and thinking—have changed.

Our modern understanding of TS developed from the writings of Jean-Marc Itard, the French neurologist who observed the Marquise de Dampierre. In 1885, the year after the marquise died, another French neurologist and former student of Itard's identified nine patients who displayed assorted bursts of movements and sounds. Dr. Georges Gilles de la Tourette compared his patients' tics with

Dr. Georges Gilles de la Tourette, a French neurologist, worked with Dr. Itard's papers as well as his own research to identify a tic disorder.

the marquise's symptoms and wrote a paper about their similarities. Because he was the first to identify a tic disorder, it was called *maladie des tics de Gilles de la Tourette* (Gilles de la Tourette tic illness) in his honor.

Dr. Gilles de la Tourette believed that patients with TS could not control their tics. He further assumed that TS ran in families. He was sure the behaviors stemmed from neurological problems (related to the nervous system) rather than psychological (emotional and behavioral) ones. But the late 1800s was a time when Dr. Sigmund Freud and his psychiatry and talk therapy were gaining popularity. Tourette worked closely with Freud and thought Freud might be able to help his patient, even though TS was understood to be a movement rather than a psychiatric problem. Tourette sent his patients to Dr. Freud.

The 1900s brought a new wave of thinking about many illnesses, including TS. A few doctors suggested that sudden head movements, throat clearing, and sniffing resulted from sinus and tonsil infections. These doctors removed the infected parts through surgery and, without proper follow-up, declared the patients cured. Many patients probably did suffer from infections. But those who actually had TS went untreated after their surgery.

Renewed interest in psychology and how the mind works led to a different understanding of TS. The condition again fell under the heading of mental illness. Psychologists and psychiatrists searched for any number of mental causes for the puzzling behaviors displayed in their offices. They claimed patients who ticced were mad or unstable. They figured some terrible secret from the patient's life was expressing itself through these outbursts. Or they blamed the family for the child's problems. Mothers, in particular, were singled out as bad parents.

The idea that mental illness caused TS and that those who had TS could somehow control their actions persisted until the late 1950s. In 1958 the drug haloperidol was manufactured and prescribed for individuals with various neurological problems. Doctors decided to give it to patients with TS. The doctors discovered that people with the disorder responded to the medication with fewer tics, thereby proving that TS was a disorder of the nervous system.

Since that time, doctors have come to realize what Gilles de la Tourette knew from the start: Tourette syndrome is a physical disorder, and people who live with it cannot control what they do and say. Yet old thinking lingers, even among some in the medical community. That's why sharing facts about this condition is so important.

IS TOURETTE SYNDROME CATCHING?

A common question for someone with Tourette syndrome is "How did I get it?" Sometimes, the question comes from a deeper concern about whether TS is contagious, or catching, like the flu. Although the exact cause of TS remains unclear, scientists do know tics and TS are never contagious. People with TS are born with a tendency toward the condition, much as they are born with a specific color of hair or eyes. This tendency may come from several different sources.

March 9, 2011

From the Pages of USA TODAY

Singing through Tourette syndrome

Among those turning heads on this season's *American Idol* is contestant James Durbin. Notable for his impressive vocal range, Durbin, 22, of Santa Cruz, Calif., has also caught viewers' attention with his frank and moving discussion about having been diagnosed with Asperger syndrome [a disorder characterized by difficulty understanding social rules and cues, and very focused interests] and Tourette syndrome.

At an *Idol* reception last week, Durbin told USA Today that he loves hearing that people are inspired by his history of overcoming adversity "because it fuels me to do better and to push myself even further."

Tourette's typically first appears in early childhood and worsens in preteen years, but it tends to ease by late adolescence, says psychology professor Douglass Woods, director of the Tic Disorder Specialty Clinic at the University of Wisconsin–Milwaukee. It peaks "when young people are most vulnerable to the challenges of early adolescence."

That was the case for Ariel Small, now 17, of Highland Park, Ill., a high school junior and football player. In middle school, the involuntary blinking, tongue thrusting, shrugging and vocalizations that had started in elementary school were met with teasing and ridicule.

"Middle school was a rough period," he says. He eventually found understanding and a sense of empowerment through a local Tourette Syndrome Association support group and training as a youth ambassador

BRAIN MESSAGES

Recent research shows that TS is a breakdown in how different parts of the brain send messages. The cerebrum is the largest portion of the brain, where language, sensation, voluntary movement, memory, emotion, and imagination impulses originate. The likely seat of the problem lies in the basal ganglia, the operating system that connects acts set into motion in the cerebrum with nerves and muscles that

to educate others about the disorder.

High school, he says, has been a very different situation, in part because "everyone has their own things to deal with and is less interested in other people's issues," but also because he has gotten involved in sports, become more social and found "a group of friends who could move past" his condition.

Dave Pittman, 29, of Mountain Home, Ark., says his tics practically disappeared in high school but intensified during college when the typical student lifestyle— "lack of sleep, bad diet, too much caffeine and stress"—was compounded by the rigors of touring as part of a Liberty University singing group.

In 2010, he too landed on *Idol*, where he had a short run in the early rounds before being cut. But Pittman's dreams of a singing career are still on track. He's working on a solo album, which is scheduled to be released in May.

"Performing is my only spot where I escape the Tourette's world," he says.

Durbin agrees. At one audition, he told the *American Idol* judges he had been diagnosed with Tourette's, but "when I sing,

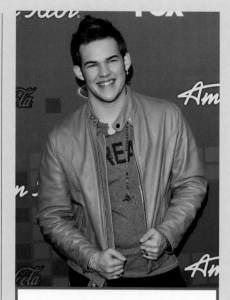

When he was on the show, *American Idol* contestant James Durbin talked about dealing with Tourette syndrome. Durbin finished fourth on the tenth season of *American Idol*.

it just all goes away. I don't have a care in the world."

—Michelle Healy

fulfill them. The basal ganglia are a group of nerve cell clusters deep within the brain that play a vital role in smooth muscle actions and stopping and starting movements.

Researchers base their claim on the fact that the basal ganglia are involved in other movement disorders, such as Parkinson's disease and Huntington's chorea. With these diseases, uncontrolled movements result from nerve cell decay. The brain produces less of the

THE HUMAN BRAIN

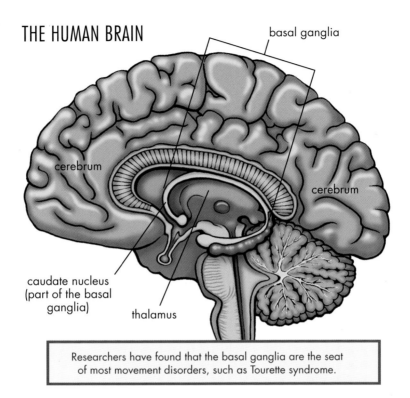

basal ganglia

cerebrum

cerebrum

caudate nucleus
(part of the basal
ganglia)

thalamus

Researchers have found that the basal ganglia are the seat of most movement disorders, such as Tourette syndrome.

neurotransmitter dopamine as the cells weaken. Neurotransmitters are brain chemicals that carry signals from one nerve cell to another. Without this communication, nerve pathways become tense, causing rigid muscles and shaky, slow movements.

Instead of a shortage of dopamine, as in Parkinson's, nerve cells in TS may produce too much dopamine and are extra sensitive to the chemical. One study from the National Institute of Mental Health identifies an area of the basal ganglia called the caudate nucleus as the source of the problem. The study compares brain scans of five pairs of identical twins who had TS. Findings show that the twin with more severe symptoms of TS displayed greater sensitivity in the caudate nucleus.

In cases of excess dopamine, the chemical floods the caudate nucleus, which reduces its ability to send messages from the brain to body parts that control movements. Dopamine overloads trigger sudden spurts of uncontrolled movements. They cause failure of the normal brake system that controls unwanted impulses to move or speak. As a result, an impulse slips past the brakes, leading to body jerks or unexpected sound. A similar response may develop from too little of the neurotransmitters serotonin and norepinephrine. A shortage of these chemicals can limit movement, which may also lead to tics.

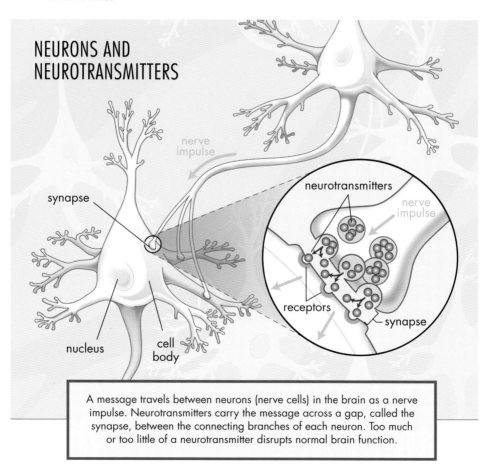

NEURONS AND NEUROTRANSMITTERS

nerve impulse

neurotransmitters

synapse

nerve impulse

receptors

synapse

nucleus

cell body

A message travels between neurons (nerve cells) in the brain as a nerve impulse. Neurotransmitters carry the message across a gap, called the synapse, between the connecting branches of each neuron. Too much or too little of a neurotransmitter disrupts normal brain function.

USA TODAY

Some scientists question whether slight differences in the brain's structure account for how nerve cells absorb chemicals. So far, studies point to differences in the size of the basal ganglia in TS patients and others. One study of twins with TS reveals that the more affected twin has a 7 percent smaller right caudate nucleus. Scientists continue to study how other parts of the brain might be involved in TS.

INFECTION

Scientists are also studying whether infection triggers TS. Normally, when infection invades the body, such as the disease-causing bacteria streptococcus, or strep, the body creates substances called antibodies to fight off the attacker. Sometimes these antibodies get confused and attack healthy tissue in addition to the infection. In other words, the body attacks itself—a response called an autoimmune reaction.

Researchers believe that a small number of TS cases may result from an autoimmune response to strep infections in which antibodies attack nervous system tissue. Damage from antibodies causes changes in the basal ganglia. When someone prone to tics contracts strep or a similar infection, symptoms tend to flare, change, or worsen. Several small studies suggest that strep antibodies account for abnormal behavior and movements in obsessive-compulsive disorder, hyperactivity, and other tic disorders. However, a 2009 study found little connection between strep infection and TS. Research on a possible strep-tic link continues.

IT'S IN THE GENES

Various studies reveal that TS runs in families. The brain's ability to regulate neurotransmitters passes from parent to child through DNA, material in each cell of the body that acts as the blueprint of life. Genes

GENETIC MATERIAL WITHIN A CELL

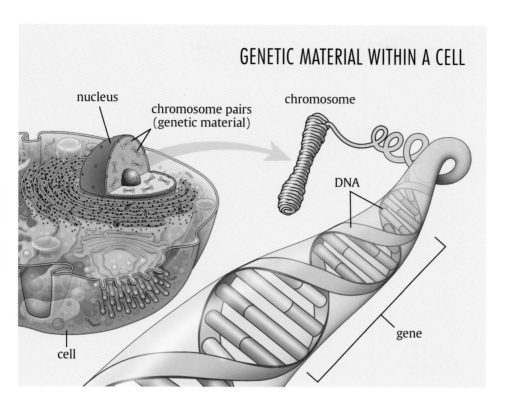

nucleus

chromosome pairs
(genetic material)

chromosome

DNA

gene

cell

are the tiny sections of DNA that control or influence traits in the body.

Babies receive a set of genes from each parent. The genes contain all the biological information their bodies will need to develop. Genes determine hair color, eye color, and other physical and mental features. Sometimes genes develop irregularities during the process of normal cell activity. Occasionally, an irregularity in one or more genes can lead to a disorder.

In the 1980s and early 1990s, scientists thought a child could inherit TS through a single gene from either parent. But researchers have greatly increased their understanding of genetics since the early 2000s. More recent studies have shown that a complex combination of genes is probably involved in causing TS.

February 22, 2011

From the Pages of USA TODAY

10 years after genome project, how did we do?

It's been 10 years since two scientific studies officially marked the completion of the human "genome"—a draft blueprint of our genes. Amid celebrations of the anniversary, experts and the public are still pondering the payoffs. What has mapping our genes meant to humanity?

Thanks to the human genome effort, we know human beings have at least 20,000 genes. Genes are what encode the recipes our cells use to churn out the proteins that our bodies build into blood, bone, brain and everything else. Genes themselves are written in DNA. DNA is made of four chemicals that pair off to create a long "double helix" structure of interwoven "base pairs." Human DNA is built of 3 billion of these base pairs.

So far, researchers have located several different genes possibly linked to TS. They believe multiple abnormal genes contribute to tic formation and other overlapping disorders. Differences in symptoms may depend on which genes are affected in a given person and how they work together. In 2006 the Tourette Syndrome Association International Consortium of Genetics completed the largest genetic linkage study to date of families affected by TS to help determine which genes influence specific TS behaviors. Results from investigations such as this one may lead to new treatments.

Even before scientists had advanced knowledge of genetics, research pointed to TS being an inherited condition. One striking study involved triplets who were born in Sweden during the 1930s.

Mapping these base pairs is what occupied the $3 billion Human Genome Project, and a private $300 million Celera effort, a competition that culminated in 2001 with releases of draft human genomes in the journals *Nature* and *Science*. Since then, researchers have sequenced genomes of dozens of people worldwide, finding clues to the origins of disease from diabetes to cancer [including some for TS]. At the same time, progress in using the genome to cure diseases has not reached all expectations.

"It's now been 10 years since humans deciphered the digital code that defines us as a species," says a review led by James Evans of the University of North Carolina–Chapel Hill, in the current *Science*. "If we fail to evaluate the considerable promise of genomics through a realistic lens, exaggerated expectations will undermine its legitimacy." The review notes a number of roadblocks to realizing the promise of genomics:

Medicine always takes longer to see treatments move from lab bench to bedside. And along the way, there can be disappointments as in hormone replacement therapy (prescribing female hormones to aging women who lose them).

People are still human. Patients still drink, smoke, overeat and underexercise, even after you tell them their genes put them at risk.

Yet, the promise of understanding the human genome is still there, the reviewers say, particularly in understanding how inherited diseases strike. With patience and mistakes along the way, they conclude, "We believe that genomic discovery . . . will provide great benefits to human health."

—*Dan Vergano*

Different families adopted each baby shortly after birth. The two girls and one boy each developed TS at the age of five, suggesting that Tourette syndrome passes from one generation to another. Forty-seven years later, the sisters and brother reunited. Interestingly, the triplets developed different tic behaviors. The man's only symptom was frequent blinking. One sister blinked and produced facial tics that traveled down her body and turned into leg kicking. The other sister displayed more severe signs: head and shoulder jerks, leg movements, facial tics, and grunts.

Twin and triplet studies offer valuable understanding of how genes and environment influence disease. The Swedish study shows the powerful role genes play in TS. But it also points to the environment as a key factor in altering the type and frequency of tics.

Studying twins can help researchers determine what role genes play in Tourette syndrome and how environmental factors may impact symptoms.

Theories abound about events occurring before and after a baby is born that may change how the brain develops. Did the brain receive too little oxygen before or during birth? Did the baby receive too few nutrients before or after birth, which would keep weight down and slow brain growth? More recent twin studies point to brain size and birth weight as predictors of more severe tics later in life. Here, too, further research continues.

WHAT IS THE GENETIC RISK FOR INHERITING TS?

One or both parents must contribute the right combination of genes for TS or related disorders for their child to reveal signs of TS. If a parent has TS, the likelihood of a child acquiring any form of mild tic, tic disorder, or obsessive-compulsive symptoms is about 56 percent for boys and 30 percent for girls. The odds of having TS serious enough to seek medical attention are much less. Even if a child displays signs of TS, chances are symptoms will be mild or nonexistent. They may vary in the type, strength, and frequency of tics. Or they may show up as obsessive-compulsive behaviors or attention and learning problems without any tics. The possibility also exists that a gene-carrying child will never develop TS symptoms. What studies show for sure is that children of one or both parents with TS have a higher than normal risk of mild tic disorders and obsessive-compulsive behaviors than those in the general population.

PEOPLE WITH TOURETTE SYNDROME

Tourette syndrome is more common than once believed. Although as many as one in one hundred Americans have TS, that number includes three to four times as many boys as girls. In fact, boys are three to five times more likely than girls to have most disorders related to learning, speech, and behavior. Not all boys with a parent who has TS will develop a serious case. But almost all will experience some tic-related behaviors during their lifetime. By comparison, girls from an at-risk family develop obsessive-compulsive symptoms more often than tics.

Scientists differ about why this is so. Some think more boys may get diagnosed because they tend to act out more, which cannot be ignored, while girls display subtler nervous habits and repeat actions, such as compulsions. Other researchers consider the physical differences between genders. Sex-related hormones, such as the main male sex hormone testosterone, may play a role in what TS symptoms boys and girls acquire. The sharp rise in hormones during adolescence could be a reason why tics seem to worsen

In families with a history of Tourette syndrome, boys are more likely than girls to develop tic-related behaviors. Scientists have different ideas about why this is the case.

during puberty and fade as hormones stabilize in the late teens and twenties. In fact, with about 20 to 30 percent of TS cases, symptoms disappear completely by adulthood.

Aside from their tics, people who live with TS are just like anyone else. They display the same range of intellect, interests, and feelings as people without Tourette disorder, and they live a normal life span.

As Jake says: "You are perfectly normal if you have TS. I bet you I could name something wrong with every person in our entire school. We just have tics we cannot help. We should never be treated differently, except maybe [to allow] for the tics."

FUTURE RESEARCH

Modern research brings up a wealth of important issues. If identical twins have the same genetic risk for TS, why does one exhibit more severe symptoms than the other? What role does environment, including pollution, infection, or stress, play in determining the severity of these behaviors?

Questions of prevention are also tied to TS research. What if scientists succeed in identifying abnormal brain patterns or genes that result in TS symptoms? Could they then eliminate TS by screening babies before they are born and treating the condition? Or could they protect children from ever being exposed to TS triggers in the environment? The challenge for the future will be to discover answers to these questions.

CHAPTER FOUR

WHAT TREATMENTS REDUCE TICS?

In his book Against Medical Advice, *James Patterson writes about a five-year-old boy named Cory who has developed uncontrollable urges to shake his head before his fifth birthday. As Cory ages, more tics rattle his body. Involuntary talking and shouting follow. Cory's body becomes increasingly explosive and unpredictable. His parents take him from doctor to doctor searching for a correct diagnosis and treatment that would lessen their child's escalating tics and emotional stress. For the next fifteen years, Cory tries a range of treatments. Often his condition worsens from different combinations of medications that merely trade one symptom for another. Cory says he feels as if he is hanging from the end of a puppeteer's string, because his body is so out of control. As Cory ages, he begins to get control of his TS symptoms. By the age of twenty-four, Cory runs an Internet business, sings in a band, and hardly takes any medication. He believes that his struggles had made him a stronger person.*

Most cases of Tourette syndrome require no treatment. Tics are so mild that they never interfere with everyday activities or cause harm to the individual. Should the tics worsen, people with moderate symptoms can usually control them by reducing stress and making minor lifestyle changes.

A small number of people, however, find that their tics interfere with daily activities enough to require treatment. For these individuals, a qualified professional can help them find a structured path to lessen their discomfort. Although Tourette syndrome has no cure, several forms of treatment are available to reduce its effects on daily life. The most effective plan for someone may involve more than one type of treatment.

MEDICATION

One of the most effective ways to calm tics is with medication. Many different drugs counter the chemical imbalance that results in TS. Not all common tic medications work for everyone, though. Some medications may reduce one tic but not another. Certain tics may get worse. Patients often try several medications before finding the correct combination of one or more medicines and doses. Even then, unwanted side effects can blunt the benefits of fewer tics. And some medicines lose their punch over time. Constant monitoring by families and physicians who know about TS is important to help kids feel their best.

Doctors most familiar with TS medications are pediatricians who treat children and adolescents, neurologists who concentrate on the nervous system, and psychiatrists who manage mental health issues. These specialists usually begin treatment by ordering low doses of medication. They suggest taking each new medicine for at least a couple weeks, until it reaches the right level in the blood to work. If

Many people with Tourette syndrome take medication to help with the symptoms. Some are on several kinds of medication at one time.

needed, a doctor will change doses or types of medicine gradually and one at a time. That way, the patient, parents, and teachers can observe reactions to the medication—good or bad. If more than one medication change occurs at a time, determining what caused which new symptom will be difficult. Some doctors recommend keeping a diary to record results of different medicines. Those records help patients, together with their physicians, decide whether or not a medication is right for them.

ANTI-TIC MEDICINES

Doctors often begin treatment with medicines that block or reduce the amount of the neurotransmitter dopamine in the brain. Neuroleptics are a common class of such medications. By suppressing dopamine, these medicines can decrease motor and vocal tics. Two frequently recommended neuroleptics are Haldol (the brand name for haloperidol) and Orap (the brand name for pimozide).

For a long time, Haldol has been the main neuroleptic prescribed, but in some patients, it proves more troublesome than tics. Some people complain of sleepiness, restlessness, or dull thinking. Others struggle with weight gain, memory loss, stiff muscles, dry mouth, blurred vision, constipation, or depression. Orap and other neuroleptics may produce similar side effects but only at higher doses. Even with these problems, many people choose to stay on medicine rather than tic.

As a teen, Mark took Haldol for almost three years. He complained of sleepiness and a huge weight gain. He couldn't stay awake in class, had dry mouth, and ate constantly. "The side effects were almost as bad as the TS," he recalled, so he tried several other medications. In two years, Mark went through seven medications. But nothing worked except Haldol. He continued on Haldol until the end of his freshman year at college. By then, his symptoms had subsided.

In rare cases, long-term treatment with neuroleptics produces tardive dyskinesia. This movement disorder involves random muscle actions, similar to TS. With tardive dyskinesia, most movements appear around the mouth, but they may spread throughout the body as slow, snakelike arm and leg motions and quick eyelid twitches. Symptoms usually but not always disappear when medicine leaves the body.

Another classification of drugs that helps control behavior symptoms is central adrenergic inhibitors. Originally, these medicines were prescribed to calm high blood pressure. Doctors noticed that they also controlled such behavior symptoms as raging and impulse control issues. A popular medication in this category is Catapres (clonidine). Catapres seems to produce fewer side effects and long-term problems than neuroleptics. Sleepiness and dry mouth, the main difficulties, lessen with time. But so does the drug's effectiveness.

A recent study indicates that nicotine eases symptoms of Tourette syndrome. Nicotine is the drug in tobacco that makes smoking addictive. It also increases manufacture of the chemical dopamine. Usually, TS symptoms come from too much dopamine. But nicotine floods the dopamine receptors enough so they shut down completely. No doctors recommend that anyone— especially children—smoke, because smoking causes a host of other problems. Rather, some doctors suggest that patients with the most severe tics try nicotine gum or patches. A patch worn directly on the skin delivers a small, even dose of nicotine. Thus, someone wearing a patch can get a gentle dose that may relieve tics on an ongoing basis.

Nicotine treatment for TS symptoms is not for everyone. Seventy percent of children who have tried the patch complain of skin irritation and nausea. Research is under way on drugs that act the same way as nicotine in the brain but will not produce unwanted side effects if used as a TS treatment. One such drug is mecamylamine, another blood pressure drug.

As doctors learn more about specific chemicals involved in TS, they experiment with a host of other medications that may serve different patients better. Information about newer medications and their effects is available from the Tourette Syndrome Association and websites mentioned in the Resources section of this book.

MEDICATIONS FOR CONDITIONS RELATED TO TS

For some children, tics are the least of their problems. Poor attention, mind-numbing obsessions, panic attacks, or mood swings may cause more trouble than classic TS symptoms. These other conditions often require greater attention to focus on activities most people take for granted. Treating one condition without worsening another can be tricky. Drugs that work best with ADHD may increase tics. Others that control tics may increase depression or obsessions. Treatment becomes a dance to calm the most serious behavior without arousing the others.

"We find that symptoms keep evolving," Adam's mother explains. "We always look at what is most serious. Is his inability to focus in class the more serious problem? Or is he about to be kicked out of school for behavior problems? Is he picking mosquito bites so ferociously that he drips blood? We constantly weigh what is worse and have him on a variety of medications based on that evaluation."

In the few cases where symptoms are linked to strep infection, the choice of medication is easy: antibiotics. For most cases, however, the choice becomes more complicated. Two main types of drugs that treat TS-related symptoms are stimulants and antidepressants. Each produces a change in one or more brain chemicals that affect behavior.

February 22, 2000

From the Pages of USA TODAY

Nicotine may relieve Tourette's

Nicotine actually appears to have a good side, although no one is advising people to take up smoking for their health. Besides hooking smokers on cigarettes, nicotine may help some brain disorders, according to research presented Monday at the annual meeting of the American Association for the Advancement of Science in Washington, D.C.

Nicotine's stigma can make it difficult to recruit research subjects, says Paul Sanberg, a neuroscientist at the University of South Florida in Tampa who studies the drug in Tourette's syndrome, which is characterized by vocal and physical tics.

In an eight-week study that has not been published, Sanberg's team randomly assigned 70 young Tourette's patients to either nicotine patches or placebo patches. On average, the patients on the nicotine patches were able to cut their dosage of Haldol, a potent tranquilizer used to treat Tourette's, by about half, Sanberg says. Haldol has a number of undesirable side effects, including learning disabilities. None of the young people became addicted to nicotine. Nausea, a slightly increased heart rate and itchiness from the patch were the main side effects.

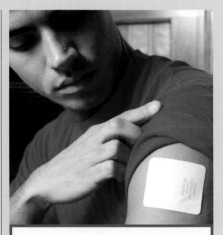

A nicotine patch can relieve tics in some people with Tourette syndrome. It can allow them to cut their dosage of the drug Haldol. Haldol often has undesirable side effects for users.

Nicotine is thought to work by regulating brain levels of chemicals involved in carrying messages between nerve cells, Sanberg says. Tourette's patients have excessive levels of dopamine in the brain, while Parkinson's disease patients don't have enough.

—Rita Rubin

May 2, 2006

From the Pages of USA TODAY

Adult antipsychotics can worsen troubles: Critics call for more research into effects on children

Evan was aggressive and hyperactive and had been diagnosed with a variety of other ailments, including obsessive-compulsive disorder. A couple of years ago, Evan was taking five psychiatric drugs, says his mother, Mary. Two were so-called atypical antipsychotics, a group of relatively new drugs approved by the Food and Drug Administration (FDA) for treating adults with schizophrenia or bipolar disorder [two psychological conditions].

"Evan was a walking zombie on all those drugs," Mary says.

Now, he has been weaned from the drugs and takes medicine only for attention-deficit disorder, she says. And he is mentally healthier than he has ever been.

Outpatient prescriptions for children ages 2 to 18 jumped about fivefold—from just under half a million to about 2.5 million—from 1995 to 2002, a survey shows. At the same time, reports of deaths and dangerous side effects potentially linked to the drugs are increasing. A USA TODAY analysis of Food and Drug Administration data shows at least 45 deaths of children from 2000 to 2004 where an atypical was considered the "primary suspect." More than 1,300 cases reported bad side

Stimulants boost the flow of norepinephrine and dopamine. This class of drugs increases energy in most people, but it calms children with ADHD, allowing them to pay attention longer and concentrate better in school. As with TS medication, however, stimulants can have unpleasant side effects. The popular drugs Ritalin or Concerta (methylphenidates) or Dexedrine (dextroamphetamine) often cause nervousness or impair sleeping and eating. When either

effects, including some that can be life threatening.

One of the most disturbing, potentially dangerous trends linked to atypicals is routinely giving kids several psychiatric drugs, says child psychiatrist Joseph Penn of Bradley Hospital and Brown University School of Medicine in Providence, R.I. "We know very little about the interaction of these drugs, the effects they could be having on kids," he says.

There has been little carefully controlled, long-term research on children taking most psychiatric drugs, including the atypical antipsychotics. The FDA is trying to get more pediatric research on the atypicals, says Thomas Laughren, the agency's director of the psychiatry products division.

Five drug companies are doing their own pediatric studies on children with disorders as diverse as ADHD, autism, conduct disorder and Tourette syndrome. The National Institute of Mental Health also is conducting pediatric studies, but the research is primarily funded and supervised by pharmaceutical companies. According to a research review published in February, 90% of drug-company-funded studies come up with findings that support the company's drug.

"The American public is operating under the illusion that a drug is safe just because it's approved by the FDA," says Jeffrey Lieberman, chairman of psychiatry at the Columbia College of Physicians and Surgeons in New York. Studies lasting a few weeks to a few months, with a couple of thousand patients total, won't reveal all that's wrong with a drug, he says.

Lieberman thinks one solution would be for the FDA to be given a new legal authority: the right to require drug companies seeking to gain approval of a drug to contribute to a collective pool at the National Institutes of Health. The NIH could supervise larger safety and effectiveness studies of medicines after they're on the market.

A national electronic medical records database that would capture all bad side effects of drugs, and require ages and diagnoses, could do a lot to protect children from careless prescribing and reveal the effects of antipsychotics, experts say.

—*Marilyn Elias*

occurs, doctors may play with the timing of doses. For example, some suggest taking medication only on school days, when paying attention in class is important.

For some patients, more serious problems occur. Stimulants may stunt body growth or trigger or increase tics. Taking regular vacations from the drug helps prevent slowed growth. For mounting tics, doctors usually recommend switching to an antidepressant.

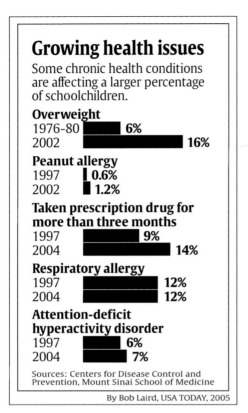

Growing health issues

Some chronic health conditions are affecting a larger percentage of schoolchildren.

Overweight
1976-80 **6%**
2002 **16%**

Peanut allergy
1997 **0.6%**
2002 **1.2%**

Taken prescription drug for more than three months
1997 **9%**
2004 **14%**

Respiratory allergy
1997 **12%**
2004 **12%**

Attention-deficit hyperactivity disorder
1997 **6%**
2004 **7%**

Sources: Centers for Disease Control and Prevention, Mount Sinai School of Medicine

By Bob Laird, USA TODAY, 2005

These medications smooth the action of neurotransmitters. They reduce the uncontrollable obsessions and compulsions from OCD and depression. But they can cause dry mouth, muscle twitches, difficulty sleeping, and drowsiness. Some children become so sleepy from these medications that they can barely climb out of bed in the morning, let alone learn.

"I was given a lot of prescription drugs that gave me bad side effects," Brian agrees. "One medication caused me to be unable to urinate [a rare side effect].... It makes a bad situation worse.... Now I take two different medications, one for anxiety attacks and one for depression. These have done wonders. Both give me an overall feeling of calm, which helps with TS."

Doctors may prescribe a combination of drugs, as in Brian's case, to balance different TS and related symptoms. With any of these medications, doctors recommend continued monitoring to prevent interactions. Moreover, they caution against mixing chemicals of any kind while on medication. Drinking alcohol, smoking, or using other drugs (whether recreationally or for medical reasons) while taking mind-altering prescription drugs can produce serious reactions. Someone taking powerful medications needs to check with his or her doctor before taking even the mildest over-the-counter cold medication.

Raymond's mother remembers what happened when her son took a cough medicine in addition to his other medications. "His blood pressure was so high he was flying, and we didn't know. He went to the school nurse because he was acting funny." To avoid such dangerous drug interactions, doctors and patients must carefully consider which medications may be used in combination.

TREATMENT WITHOUT MEDICATION

DIET

Doctors differ about how much diet affects TS behavior. A few physicians favor strict diets that limit certain types of foods, while others suggest that food has nothing to do with how someone behaves. Yet many parents report changes in their child after several weeks of limiting specific foods. Common problem foods are sugary snacks, junk foods (such as potato chips, white bread, fried treats), dairy products, caffeinated drinks, chocolate, and tomatoes. Most often, parents notice a decrease in their hyper child's activity level.

Eating a lot of junk food such as chips, cookies, and candy can often increase hyperactivity in children with Tourette syndrome.

In some cases, a food allergy produces changes in behavior. There are two ways to test for food allergies. One is to eat a limited diet—only foods that rarely cause allergic reactions—for a couple of weeks. Then add one food at a time, watching for behavior changes. Another method is for two weeks, avoid eating food that is suspected of causing problems. Add the questionable food and see if symptoms increase. If they do, eliminate that food from the diet. Otherwise, eat what is generally healthful for the body without adding food obsessions to the list of TS complications.

VITAMINS AND FOOD SUPPLEMENTS

Usually, the body manufactures the balance of vitamins it needs to run smoothly. Some researchers believe that when the body's systems are out of whack, as with TS, extra vitamins can help restore balance and reduce signs of disorder. But specialists differ about the effectiveness of taking vitamins or any food supplements.

Many critics question taking the large doses of vitamins recommended for certain results. High doses of over-the-counter supplements taken without a doctor's supervision can cause serious disease that may go unnoticed. And recent studies indicate that supplements once thought harmless may also interact with prescription medications, causing other health problems. In addition, vitamins and supplements require no prescription and are not government regulated. So studies about their effects and interactions with other drugs are limited. Without government testing, no agency assures dosages and purity of the products, as with prescription medication.

One of the more common supplements thought beneficial for TS-related disorders is vitamin B6. Vitamin B6 helps many chemicals in the brain work. Although some families report success with vitamin B6 and other nutrients, including blue-green algae, no formal studies verify these results. More research is needed in this area.

Caroline's mother recalls, "We've tried nutritional supplements." Caroline also tried a special diet. "We thought these things might be helping for a while, but we think it was more the medication than the supplements." Vitamins and supplements remain an option for TS patients trying to decrease their symptoms.

SURGERY

Around the year 2000, Belgian surgeons began testing a new surgical technique to reduce severe movement from neurological conditions. Deep brain stimulation (DBS) involves surgically implanting a battery-operated device with electrodes into the brain. The device sends high-frequency electrical charges into the site of the excess brain activity that causes tics. By charging different parts of the basal ganglia or thalamus, doctors find they can locate spots that control motor and vocal tics. Over time, they repeat the charges until tics fade.

Doctors look at an image of the brain as they perform deep brain stimulation surgery on a patient with Parkinson's disease. DBS is a possible treatment for adults who have TS with severe tics.

DBS received U.S. government approval as a way to reduce tremors and stiffness from Parkinson's disease in 2002 and as a treatment for OCD in 2009. Researchers continue to study its potential to treat TS, with the first controlled study confirming its effectiveness published in 2007. But most physicians view DBS as a last resort for when tics refuse to respond to other treatments.

Surgery for neurological disorders is controversial among those in the medical community, especially in the United States. Surgery can cause complications such as bleeding, stroke, and infection. And doctors don't know if repeated electric charges will cause long-term side effects. Brain stimulation may cause changes in behavior—in mood, movements, sensations, or thinking—that have not been documented yet.

As yet, no studies have focused on DBS for children with TS. Doctors wait to see if children outgrow their tics, as many do, before considering the procedure. This treatment is currently considered experimental and only for extreme cases in adults until further studies are completed.

BOTOX INJECTIONS

Botox (onabotulinumtoxinA) is a poisonous protein that acts on the nervous system. Injections of the protein into specific muscle groups either weaken or paralyze them. In the early 1980s, eye doctors began using Botox injections to relax imbalanced eye muscles that caused the eyeball to cross, resulting in blurred vision. The U.S. government later approved the technique for other medical conditions, such as severe sweating, bladder control, and spastic movements. The injections gained popularity among anyone who wanted to relax muscles that contribute to wrinkles.

By the mid-2000s, doctors tried the injections for muscle groups involved in tics from TS. Usually neurologists or otolaryngologists

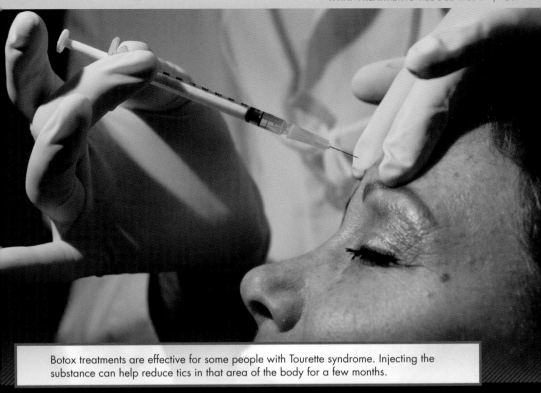

Botox treatments are effective for some people with Tourette syndrome. Injecting the substance can help reduce tics in that area of the body for a few months.

(doctors specializing in the ears, nose, and throat) performed these injections. They discovered that for some people, Botox injections reduced or eliminated tics for three or four months before the patients needed repeat injections. The injections appeared to lessen the urge to tic as well as the actual burst of muscle movement. For example, Botox injections to the vocal cords proved effective for reducing extreme vocal tics.

Although promising, doctors warn of certain drawbacks. Botox treatment targets only specific muscle groups, such as the vocal cords, the neck, parts of the face, or extremities. The treatment is not a remedy for more generalized tics. Botox is poisonous, so the body can safely handle only so much of it at a time. Other side effects, including weakened muscle groups at the injection site, may cause concern. In some instances, patients injected with Botox to ease vocal tics have wound up with lower voice volume.

April 21, 2003

From the Pages of USA TODAY

The little neurotoxin that could

It was originally approved for medical use in the USA 14 years ago to treat crossed eyes and uncontrollable blinking. Today, it has been used by more than 2.5 million people in 70 countries to treat a wide variety of conditions. It can help children with cerebral palsy [a condition that causes impaired movement] walk. It can end migraines [severe headaches]. It can greatly diminish the physical tics associated with Tourette syndrome and has been used to treat the severely obese. And this week, British scientists announced that it might treat the chronic pain of cancer.

Not bad for something normally associated with frivolous self-involvement. Because the drug in question is the botulinum toxin, commonly sold in the USA as Botox.

It may indeed be the friend of aging starlets with its wrinkle-reducing powers. But it also is the deadliest neurotoxin on the planet, able to destroy nerve and muscle function in tiny doses. And it's a

COGNITIVE BEHAVIOR THERAPY

Many children who have TS with obsessions benefit from cognitive behavior therapy. With this treatment, a trained therapist works with the patient to track unwanted behaviors such as excessive hand washing. The patient records each time he or she feels the compulsion, noting particular situations that trigger the action. Then the therapist helps the patient recognize the triggers and anticipate feeling the urge to wash his or her hands. The therapist may suggest more acceptable behaviors to perform instead of hand washing or ways to counteract the urge. This method helps patients retrain the brain to react differently to trigger situations.

"Cognitive therapy helped me become more aware of my tics,"

biochemical miracle worker that stops nerves from being able to contract muscles for months at a time.

The first doctor to test the toxin on humans was Alan Scott of the Smith-Kettlewell Eye Research Institute in San Francisco in 1977. He was looking for a treatment for lazy eye, in which one set of eye muscles is hyperactive and crosses the eyes. A decade later, Canadian eye doctor Jean Carruthers, who was using the toxin to treat eye twitches, noticed that her patients looked more relaxed. With her husband, skin doctor Alastair Carruthers, she published her findings on its use in the treatment of facial wrinkles in 1989, the same year the Food and Drug Administration first approved it for treating crossed and twitching eyes.

Next, skin doctors began to notice that when their now wrinkle-free patients returned for follow-up treatments, about two-thirds reported that they'd also stopped having migraines. Today, doctors treat increasing numbers of migraine patients with Botox. Treatments are needed every three to four months.

Botox also has been used to help people with Tourette syndrome, who are beset by tics and spasms.

"Somebody with Tourette's gets a funny tingling, burning sensation in their neck, and the only way they can relieve that is to shrug their shoulder or bend their head backwards," says Major Marc DiFazio, a pediatric neurologist at Walter Reed Medical Center in Washington, D.C.

Researchers believe it is that initial tingling sensation that sets the patients off. By giving them Botox, researchers were able to help the patient's nervous system short-circuit the initial sensation. The tics decreased markedly in some patients.

—*Elizabeth Weise*

Raymond believes. Now he is aware of when he needs to raise his hand in class and how much anxiety he can stand before he is forced to do it at inappropriate times. When the urge to ask an unrelated question arises, Raymond sits on his hand. He began by learning to raise his hand every other time instead of every time. He still works on improving.

BIOFEEDBACK

People tone their body through exercise. Some therapists claim that children and adults can tone the brain through biofeedback. This training program enhances awareness of the body's automatic and unconscious processes so they can be controlled. Biofeedback is not a common tool for treating TS directly, but it has been shown to relieve stress-related conditions. With biofeedback, the patient sits at a computer or other monitoring device. Small sensors run from the patient's scalp and body to the computer. While a therapist leads the patient through mental exercises, the machine relays physical information, such as muscle tension or heart rate, back to the individual. Gradually, patients learn to connect these cues with how they feel. They learn to recognize the feeling and re-create it or change it themselves.

Some therapists credit brain exercises with improving attention and general behavior. Others counter that anybody would improve with the amount of time and attention biofeedback requires. And the cost is high. A full course of treatment includes twenty to forty hours for between $700 and $3,400, depending upon the number of hours needed and the cost of different programs. And the patient has to be willing to sit still and concentrate.

Cognitive behavior therapy and biofeedback have been credited with helping people with Tourette syndrome learn to control tics.

PSYCHOTHERAPY

Some patients with TS find psychotherapy helpful. Psychotherapy uses communication, both verbal and nonverbal (e.g., role playing or drawing pictures), with a therapist to treat mental and behavior disorders. Treatment does not involve physical intervention, such as medication, of any kind. Although Tourette syndrome does not result from psychological problems, psychotherapy can help with social and emotional problems that accompany TS, such as depression and anxiety. And it can provide support for coping with TS.

CHAPTER FIVE

TS AT HOME AND AT SCHOOL

By the time Jake was in second grade, his shoulders shrugged and his hands flicked uncontrollably, in addition to the clicking sounds he made with his mouth. At night, his body twitched and jerked for hours before allowing him to fall asleep. Without enough sleep, Jake had trouble getting up for school and often felt drowsy in class. After he was diagnosed with Tourette syndrome, staying awake grew even more difficult due to medication that caused drowsiness as a side effect.

Over the next few years, Jake's involuntary movements changed. His head jerked. His sounds became louder. Jake was less able to sit still and concentrate. For years he had liked school and earned good grades. By fifth grade, however, he found it hard to focus.

By junior high, Jake hated school. He rarely picked up social clues from other people about how to act or react. He viewed anyone trying to help him or tell him what to do as a threat. He said teachers annoyed him. He picked fights. Quick to anger, he beat up kids who crossed him or mentioned his tics.

At home, Jake argued with his parents and seldom finished his schoolwork. He carefully lined up clothes in his room, even organized his sister's closet. But he couldn't remember to pack the right papers and books needed for homework. If he completed the work, he usually forgot it at home. Rather than ask for help, Jake either blew up or shut down completely. His life became a constant struggle.

AT HOME

The effects of Tourette syndrome extend beyond the person who has it. The condition alters relationships with parents, brothers and sisters, teachers, and classmates.

PARENTS

Parents naturally want the best for their children. They may imagine their offspring's bright future. These visions probably don't include tics. Hearing a diagnosis of TS unleashes a jumble of emotions. Many parents who have been searching for answers feel relieved to discover their child has a real medical disorder. For them, the process of finding help can begin. But other parents feel guilt for passing on genes for TS and anger at the unfair blow to their family. They may think they are bad parents or worry that others judge them as either overprotective or unable to control their child.

"People make judgments about the child and parenting based solely on what they see," Aaron's mother admits. "They think that TS is just a tic, noises, or swear words. But it is so many things and so invasive. It's vague and hard to explain. You don't have the same kind of understanding and support as when you have a child in a wheelchair. With TS, your child has kind of an invisible disability."

Parents often feel frustrated that their child seems lax about school. They may struggle to understand that their child is not careless or lazy but unable to focus

Parents may not understand why their child with Tourette syndrome isn't able to focus on schoolwork. Frustrations can pile up for parents of children with TS.

because of TS and related disorders. Between coaxing their child to work, visiting doctors frequently, and learning about TS and explaining it to others, most parents are simply exhausted.

Yet parents are key to helping someone with TS progress. They can create a climate of support at home. They can engineer ways to reduce their child's stress, which lessens tics. For example, they may choose to take their child to movie theaters at times when few viewers attend to help lessen anxiety. Or they might plan quick routes to bathrooms or outdoors so kids have a place to retreat to when their tics disturb others in public places.

"We came to realize that certain situations don't work for us," Aaron's mother adds. "So we don't put ourselves in them. With Aaron, behavior issues from his ADHD make sitting still in a restaurant difficult for him." Going to long shows or to temple or church also caused problems, she says. "We accept limitations and say this doesn't work for us."

Often the parents' main job involves listening to their child, trying to figure out what actions and words really mean. For example, one mother wanted to stop her son from raging when she refused to take him shopping. Instead of saying yes or no right away to his request, she listened and parroted

One of the most important jobs of a parent of someone with TS is making sure the child feels understood.

what she heard back to her son. That way, he knew she understood correctly. As her son talked more, he revealed that his real problem was getting stuck, or obsessing, on going to buy an item. He felt worse about having this obsession than about not being allowed to go to the store. Once he felt understood, his tension subsided and the rages calmed.

When children feel supported and accepted, they learn to deal with TS better. They realize that home is a safe place to tic and relieve tension. Moreover, children who have supportive parents learn that they are much more than just their tics. They are individuals with many skills that will develop as they age.

Aaron's mother explains that she wants to be a good model for her son. "If you can't cope with what he has, how can he? You have to tell your child, '[You are] a fantastic person. And yes, you have a lot of things to cope with. But you are coping with them, and I am glad you are.'"

SISTERS AND BROTHERS

When one sibling has TS, it distorts the normal relationship between sisters and brothers. Siblings commonly bicker and compete for attention. But such rivalry can be even stronger when TS is involved.

Siblings without TS understandably become angry if a brother or a sister suddenly punches them or grunts during TV shows. They are frustrated with a sibling who plows through game boards or breaks toys. They may resent the extra attention TS requires and hate the worry and uproar it causes the family. Before a diagnosis is made, they may punch back at siblings or yell at their sibling with TS to stop making noises. Once the diagnosis is confirmed, they may feel guilty for being angry at someone with a medical problem.

Sibling reactions differ with age and the extent to which TS disrupts family routines. For younger children, jealousy is a common reaction to feeling neglected. They may imitate their brother or sister with TS to get attention or worry that they somehow caused the tics. Sometimes, siblings believe that because they do not have TS, their problems are not worth mentioning. Instead, they either try to be perfect or to cause trouble to get their parents' attention. Each approach usually leads to resentment. If parents overprotect the child with TS, siblings may resent being blamed for conflicts between the two or being held to a higher standard. If parents never explain TS, siblings worry that something more serious has happened to their sister or brother.

"I thought my brother was going to die," a twenty-four-year-old sibling remembered. "My parents whispered about [my brother's] condition behind closed doors. Nobody told me anything. I could have been more supportive when we were in junior high and high school if I'd only known what was going on. I thought he was [ticcing] on purpose."

As children mature, they may feel embarrassed about living with someone who behaves in an unusual way. Preteens and teens, in particular, often try to fit in, rarely wanting to call attention to themselves. Being with someone who tics wildly or makes noises is like wearing a neon sign that screams, "Look at me!" So sisters and brothers of Tourette patients might refuse to be seen with their sibling or to go on family outings. They don't invite friends home. They may also worry that TS is catching. And many live in fear of physical harm from a sibling who rages.

Brian recalls, "I gave my brother a lot of verbal abuse for the littlest things. For the most part it was me yelling, making a fool of myself. There were times I was so out of control, however, that I saw horror in his eyes. He cried sometimes. It doesn't make me feel good that my own brother was afraid of me."

Parents play the biggest role in helping siblings get along. If parents practice patience and understanding, sisters and brothers are more likely to do the same. Part of understanding comes with learning about TS. Knowing why a sibling behaves a certain way reduces fears and resentment. In addition, facts arm siblings with answers to questions from friends and classmates. Booklets and videos from support organizations such as the Tourette Syndrome Association can help siblings learn about TS and share this information with others.

Another important factor in family harmony is communication. A good way to foster open communication is to hold regular family meetings. Weekly meetings give all members of the family a place to air their feelings and concerns. They provide a time when everyone listens without judgment. After everyone has a say, the family can discuss solutions to problems together. As one younger sibling of a brother with TS notes, "It's important to get each person's perspective—both sides of the story. Talking things out makes living together better." If verbal communication proves difficult, individuals involved in a problem can role-play, taking one another's part. Trying to view the situation from another person's perspective can help create understanding. In addition, seeing how someone else looks acting like another family member often triggers humor, which reduces tension.

Besides meetings, parents need to schedule regular time for each child. Spending undivided time with parents lets children know they are special. During these times, parents can reassure each child of their love and resolve to keep them and their belongings safe when TS causes destructive behavior. Parents can help siblings understand that TS behaviors are the problem, not their sister or brother. Parents could talk about their own frustrations with TS and what they do to feel better. When siblings feel heard and understood, many resent their sibling with TS less and begin to value them for who they are.

Professor Peter Hollenbeck, of Purdue University in Indiana, recounts that his older brothers made fun of everything—everything but his tics. According to a newsletter from the Tourette Syndrome

Association, "Being treated like any other little brother gave [him] the self-confidence he needed to face people who were not always so accepting."

GETTING HELP OUTSIDE THE HOME

SUPPORT GROUPS

People often wonder how someone with TS could escape diagnosis for so long. For many who tic, the answer is clear. They were born that way. Tics are part of them, so they never knew that their behavior was part of a condition or that it had a specific name. Since most people with TS see extremes portrayed in the media or books, they never connect themselves with those images. A diagnosis of TS can be a shock. Individuals with the condition may question what to do next.

Joining a support group helps someone who tics to balance feelings of isolation and feeling different. People with TS share similar experiences. In a support group, they see others who struggle with tics and still succeed—in school, with friends, and on the job. They are no longer alone.

The same holds true for parent and sibling support groups. Only someone who has experienced something similar can understand the frustrations of living with a child who has TS. Parents can compare medications and techniques for handling behaviors. They can speak openly about feelings of guilt and helplessness at not being able to prevent or cure their child's tics.

"I thought I was the only one who had a kid that has TS," Jake's mother remembers. "I wondered what I did to my kid. I met this woman at the group who said this is a normal reaction from parents. I felt relieved."

Support groups can help siblings learn ways to deal with any

Support groups can help children with Tourette syndrome deal with their symptoms and worries. Families of people with TS can also benefit from attending a support group.

embarrassment they may feel from living with someone who acts differently. Siblings may discover practical options for handling a brother or sister who swears or throws things. TS groups reduce feelings of isolation from families who seem more normal. Families can find various support groups through their doctor or local Tourette Syndrome Association.

PROFESSIONAL THERAPY

When Tourette syndrome causes families to spin out of control, they need to seek professional help. Individual therapy with a licensed psychologist, psychiatrist, or social worker who has experience with TS can help family members sort through their feelings. The therapist can help the child with TS learn methods of getting along better with others. Therapy can also help other family members identify ways to help themselves when TS becomes overwhelming.

Family therapy, where everyone meets with a therapist together, puts the entire family on the same track. A therapist pinpoints when family members get stuck in routines that interfere with helpful communications. All members learn to work toward common goals as everyone assumes responsibility for how they behave.

TS GOES TO SCHOOL

Children with mild tics find that their TS rarely interferes with the ability to handle schoolwork. But school can be a nightmare for those with frequent tics or other related problems. Embarrassment can result from the inability to sit still and stay quiet; medication that causes sleepiness, nausea, and dizziness; and the lack of problem solving, organizing, and social skills. Add possible learning disabilities, obsessions, compulsions, mood swings, and rage attacks, and school can feel more like a battleground than a place to learn.

SCHOOLWORK BLUES

Take reading, for example. How many people could read a long paragraph while their head jerks? Could they understand the paragraph if they had to count the number of *A*s in each sentence? How could they finish in the allotted time when their need to read each letter in order forces them to start over repeatedly? What about writing with hand and arm tics or blinking eyes?

Math offers another challenge. Some people with TS have an obsession about a certain number. They fear that writing or reading the number will cause something awful to happen. Who could complete a test while following rituals to avoid this number? How can they convince a teacher they want to cooperate but are stuck with a notion in their head that refuses to go away?

Jake's struggles in school were typical for a child with TS. "Paying attention was an effort for Jake," his mother says. "He said his mind wandered. His handwriting was so bad his tests were illegible. Teachers would give work back. He had trouble taking notes, listening, and being able to take tests. It was overwhelming for him." Changing classes was overwhelming too. Jake took a while to settle down for each class period, and he often lost his books. He didn't write assignments in his calendar, which created more problems.

TOURETTE SYNDROME AND SCHOOL LAW

The law guarantees all children equal access to education. But until recently, TS was not covered under the federal Individuals with Disabilities Education Act (IDEA), the law that requires schools to provide education to any student with a disability in the least restrictive environment. Some states allowed TS to be covered by IDEA language that includes "other health impairments." But with school budgets shrinking, school boards tried to limit the number of special accommodations for students whom school personnel handle.

In 2011 that changed. The Tourette Syndrome Association worked with lawmakers to have TS included in the act. That means TS is confirmed by law as a neurological disorder, rather than only a behavior disorder. As a result, schools must provide appropriate education and accommodations for all students with TS.

EXPLAINING TOURETTE SYNDROME

How students with TS receive their education varies, depending on the severity of TS. Most children with TS can learn in regular classes. Some benefit from going to a resource room for part of the day. There, a specially trained teacher works with a few students at a time. Resource teachers adapt regular classroom assignments and help students organize what they learn. When needed, they support individuals in their regular classes.

If students require constant support, such as for extreme behavior problems, the school district may hire an aide to follow and assist them from class to class. If students are still unable to handle a regular classroom, they may be referred to a special needs class or a special school in a different building. Such placements are made according to specific guidelines with input from teachers, parents, and the school psychologist. In rare cases, parents decide to teach their child at home. The idea is to find a setting in which each child learns best.

November 10, 1999

From the Pages of USA TODAY

Learning disabilities no barrier to college: Tutors, textbook tapes, time management and note takers help academic stars shine

Imagine a brainstorm: colorful ideas chaotically careening through space, sometimes jettisoning off on a tangent, some crashing into each other, some overlapping. Now capture it and splat it onto a piece of paper.

Welcome to Jonathan Mooney's academic experience. And we're not talking recreational drug use here; we're talking English lit. Colored pencils are essential tools in the writing process for Mooney, a senior at Brown University [in Rhode Island], just as quiet talks with his girlfriend are a—if not the—major component of reading comprehension.

Diagnosed with dyslexia at the

Usually, minor changes and extra aid are enough to help someone with tics or learning and attention problems succeed. The first step is educating school personnel about TS. Uninformed teachers may believe that a child with TS tics on purpose. Because kids often hide or delay expressing their tics, adults assume they can be controlled.

Parents can do their part by alerting teachers that a child has TS and explaining that it is a neurological condition that cannot be controlled. In addition, parents should suggest that teachers ignore tics and devise ways to reduce triggers in class. For their part, teachers need an extra dose of patience and creativity to

elementary level, Mooney, 22, spells on a third-grade level and reads with the lowest 10% of the population. Yet at the Ivy League school, he chose to major in English and has maintained a 4.0 grade-point average.

"The myth that learning-disabled students are somehow less intelligent and therefore less able to go to college, or to go to the Ivy Leagues, needs to be debunked," says Susan Pliner, assistant dean at Brown and head of disability services.

Oh, did we mention that Mooney has a book contract with a major publishing house? And that his tutoring program, which matches learning-disabled students from Brown with elementary-age children with similar learning styles, may go national soon?

Today, students diagnosed with problems, such as dyslexia and [ADHD], face a college scene less stigmatized and much more promising than that of a generation ago.

"Colleges are much more understanding of the necessity of giving accommodations," says Carol Loewith, president of the Independent Educational Consultants Association. "If a student has been successful in high school with extended time on tests or textbooks on tape, the colleges don't consider that an excuse anymore. It's just the way the student gets information best."

"Colleges are starting to recognize that they always had students with learning disabilities or attention deficits and those students have often been their best and brightest," says Frank Sopper, dean of admissions at Landmark College in Putney, Vt.

The key to success, experts agree, is for students to fully comprehend their disabilities so they can ask for and get the support necessary to compete.

—*Karen Thomas*

work with TS students. The Tourette Syndrome Association and other associations listed in the Resources section of this book offer booklets for teachers that describe symptoms and suggest ways to manage TS and related symptoms in the classroom.

Each year, Adam's mom sends a letter to his teachers before school begins. "I lay out what his strengths and symptoms are and update what kind of medication he takes and how it affects him," she says. "I share what has worked in the past and urge teachers to call me if there are any problems. Some parents prefer to be there and talk to the teacher the first day of school, and that works well. But for us the letter works."

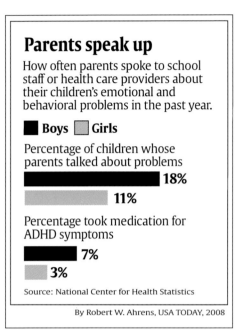

Parents speak up

How often parents spoke to school staff or health care providers about their children's emotional and behavioral problems in the past year.

■ **Boys** ▨ **Girls**

Percentage of children whose parents talked about problems

18%

11%

Percentage took medication for ADHD symptoms

7%

3%

Source: National Center for Health Statistics

By Robert W. Ahrens, USA TODAY, 2008

Many parents worry that their child with TS will be teased by classmates. If their child agrees, parents may ask teachers to talk with classmates about TS or offer to do it themselves. In some cases, learning about TS is enough to stop bullying. But merely having information does not automatically bring friends. Raymond remembers, "When I was diagnosed, my teacher sat in front of the whole class and said 'Raymond has TS, and this is what it is.'" He decided that anyone who didn't accept his TS wasn't worth befriending anyway.

BUILDING SUCCESS INTO LEARNING

Many ideas may lessen the impact of TS symptoms on learning. The following factors can help someone with TS to be successful in school:

Seating. Teachers can help students with Tourette syndrome by asking them where they want to sit. Students with frequent tics may prefer a desk in the back where others cannot see the movements or be as bothered by noises. Or they may choose to sit near the door, so they can leave if the urge to tic becomes overpowering. If paying attention is a problem, they may benefit from sitting away from windows and doorways at a desk with a clear view of the teacher. Desks should be free of unnecessary materials and nearby walls cleared of anything distracting. Some students find they can work better with a portable screen or a divider around their desk or in another room to block out unnecessary distractions.

Special signals. Agreed-upon signals can help students with TS and their teachers communicate without interrupting classes. Teachers may say code words or use hand signals to remind the student to pay attention. Similarly, students might touch an ear or raise two fingers to signal the need to be excused when the urge to tic becomes too strong and they feel a need to move around. Teacher and student can prearrange a safe place where the student can go to tic.

Timing and tests. Constant tics take time and can be tiring. Short breaks during intense work periods reduce the strain of holding back the urge to tic. Untimed tests, which also reduce stress, make up for the extra time it takes to tic. Many students ask to take tests in a private room. By being alone, they aren't wasting energy trying to suppress tics that disturb other students.

Transitions. Teachers can help students manage changes in routine by reminding them what is going to happen before the change takes place. Children who find transitions difficult work better with established routines. A written list of tasks for the day—for example, in an assignment book—lets the student check off each activity or project as it occurs. Parents and teachers can work together to review directions and items needed to complete homework assignments. The more structure

Taking a test alone in a quiet room can help children with Tourette syndrome concentrate.

January 15, 2004

From the Pages of USA TODAY

Obsessive-compulsive disorder: Early intervention helps kids get treatment before rituals are ingrained

At age 8, Elyse Monti of East Greenwich, RI, was staying up half the night to do homework. It's not that her teachers were piling it on. It's that in Elyse's mind, it had to be perfect. Elyse has obsessive-compulsive disorder, OCD, an anxiety disorder that affects about 1% of children and about 2.3% of adults.

Her father was alert to the symptoms because he has OCD himself. Her parents took her to a doctor for evaluation, and she began weekly therapy. Her symptoms abated but recur with major life changes. Upon entering high school, "I felt I had so much work to do. I didn't take time to eat. I was out of control," says Elyse, 17. Her worried parents sought help, and Elyse was hospitalized for three weeks.

to the school day, the easier it is for a disorganized student to manage.

Adjusted assignments. Students with TS need some slack in completing their tasks and should not be punished for turning in homework late. Those who have ADHD require simple and easy-to-follow instructions. Tasks should be assigned one at a time and then completed before moving to the next task. Too much work assigned together can be overwhelming, so teachers may need to reduce assignments or break them into smaller parts. For example, half a page of science questions or every other math problem on a page is easier to handle than an entire page and may be enough to reinforce a concept. For major projects, the teacher or the parent can work with the student to complete one step at a time until the entire job is done.

Researchers at the hospital have developed a form of cognitive behavior therapy, CBT, that is being used successfully to help children as young as 5. Young patients are encouraged, gently and over time, to confront whatever it is that they fear.

Often, medication can help. The medication "allow the child to do internal behavioral therapy and provide stress relief," says pediatrician Susan Swedo of the National Institute of Mental Health. But treatment can't begin unless there is a diagnosis. Early diagnosis is important because therapy is more effective before rituals and obsessions become entrenched.

People with OCD know "what they're experiencing doesn't make sense," says Swedo. "They are frightened and try to hide it as long as possible. People may spend six or seven hours a day on their rituals, and nobody knows."

Elyse was given help at an early age, but she kept her condition a secret until her sophomore year of high school, when she was assigned to write a personal essay and read it aloud in English class.

"I thought this would be a good time to come out about my OCD," Elyse says. The responses from friends "were all so positive. People said: 'If there's anything I can do,' or 'You were strong to come out about it.'"

Buoyed by the support, Elyse has become an advocate for awareness of OCD in teens and children and is active in the Obsessive-Compulsive Foundation, a national research and support group.

Her OCD is "not completely gone," she says. "There's always an event that triggers it. Last year, it was the SATs." Her medication was adjusted for a week, "then the SATs were over, and I was fine. But I know there are still bumps in the road."

—Anita Manning

Students can learn to break assignments into smaller tasks themselves. One way is to cut or fold worksheets into sections to work on one problem in each. Markers are helpful to highlight or color-code important information or different subjects. When reading long sections, students can isolate one line of text at a time by cutting a rectangle the height and width of one line from a larger piece of thick paper or cardboard. The cutout helps wandering eyes focus on words inside the opening while blocking out the rest of the page.

Taking notes can be a problem for students who cannot concentrate or write quickly. Some teachers assign a note-taking partner who can share copies of notes and assignments. For students unable to focus, other teachers prepare notes, highlighted copies of textbook pages, or samples of what they want, such as completed math problems or answered questions. To avoid homework struggles at home, parents sometimes hire a homework buddy or a professional tutor so the student can keep up with the class. Taking directions from a peer often works better than from a parent.

Learning aids. Technology and a little inventiveness provide many aids for students while in the classroom.

- Calculators reduce carelessness in solving math problems.
- Computers help students who have poor handwriting.

Using a computer or a calculator in class or to help with homework can make school easier for children living with Tourette syndrome.

- Headsets block out distracting sounds while working independently.
- Handheld audio recorders can record a lesson when students cannot focus or write quickly enough to take notes. Many teachers allow students with unreadable handwriting to record test answers.
- Recorded books enable students to absorb a text more easily if they have head jerks, obsessions, or constantly blinking eyes that make reading difficult. A recording that beeps at regular intervals can jog them out of a daydream or keep them from getting stuck on a thought or a word.
- A foam rubber mat placed on top of the desk can keep tapping tics from making much noise.
- Graph paper, or notebook paper turned sideways, helps students write numbers for math problems in straight columns.
- Color-coded folders or separators for three-ring binders organize papers for different subjects.
- Having two sets of textbooks, one to keep in class and one to keep at home, relieves the problem of remembering to bring the correct book home or back to class. Extra sets of school supplies at each location also guard against forgetting.

Students need to learn how to be their own advocates at school. If something does not work for them, they need to ask parents and teachers for help. Although symptoms of TS may make school harder, it need not be impossible. A little creativity goes a long way toward making learning easier.

CHAPTER SIX

LEARNING TO LIVE WITH TOURETTE SYNDROME

When Raymond turned five, he started sniffing and clicking his tongue. His parents took him to the doctor, who gave Raymond allergy tests and medication. But the sniffing continued. Another doctor decided he had a hole in his nose and operated. Still, Raymond kept sniffing. Without clear-cut answers, his mother insisted he sniffed on purpose to annoy her. She yelled at him to stop.

Then Raymond began licking his arm. After that followed head jerking, blinking, and, most embarrassing, grabbing his genitals. After another round of doctor's visits, Raymond learned that he had Tourette syndrome. By this time, he was ten years old and other kids noticed his uncontrolled actions.

"I would get teased constantly," Raymond remembered at the age of seventeen. "I had a really bad time. People wouldn't even ask why I was doing these things. They just made fun of me. Some seemed scared. I'd hear them talking about me behind my back. A lot of times I cried. And I acted out and hit kids."

Symptoms changed as Raymond grew older. His hands and toes jerked, and his fingers tapped on desks and tabletops. He repeated phrases other people said. He made unusual sounds with his mouth. Although normally a good student, Raymond found organizing his work increasingly more difficult by junior high. He seemed to lose the ability to set priorities. He often forgot his homework. He became unusually anxious in stressful situations and couldn't concentrate. Test taking triggered grunts and smacking noises, which bothered classmates.

In seventh grade, Raymond developed habits he could not break. His TS symptoms by then included certain compulsions. At home he *asked questions, even when he already knew the answers. At school he raised his hand in class whether or not he had an answer or a question. Raymond could figure out problems by himself, but he needed to ask questions that others found obvious. Teachers thought he took up too much class time. Classmates found him weird and made fun of him. Throughout junior high school, he had almost no friends.*

Everything improved for Raymond in high school. The school counselor helped him learn to organize his time better. He was allowed to take tests in another room or without time limits when his sounds or movements interfered with working. Raymond's grades, especially in math, soared. But the biggest difference came from finding friends who didn't make fun of him. Gradually, Raymond gained confidence. He joined the school soccer team and ran track off-season.

Playing soccer is one way for children with Tourette syndrome to get exercise and make friends. Exercise can help control tics in some people with TS.

May 12, 2004

From the Pages of USA TODAY

Parents plant encouraging seeds to learn: Nurturing produces the brainpower and willpower to grow to the fullest

Ann Chi, of Terre Haute, Indiana, is one of 20 students named to USA Today's All-USA High School Academic First Team. The high school seniors, who receive trophies and $2,500, were selected from 1,606 nominees for their scholarship, leadership and willingness to extend their abilities to benefit society. Forty more students were named to Second and Third Teams.

By any measure, the First Team members exhibit a lot of brainpower, with a combined unweighted grade-point average of 3.97 on a 4.0 scale. Beyond succeeding in academic realms, First Team members have applied their talents in a variety of ways, from concert pianist and violinist Benjamin Lee of Hudson (Ohio) High, who started a StringCoach music mentoring program, to Lisa Glukhovsky of New Milford (Conn.)

He still jerked his head sometimes or made strange sounds, but he learned to mask these movements to look more natural. For example, he sat on his hand in class when the urge to ask an unnecessary question hit. Some tics, like rubbing his crotch, went away, only to be replaced by leg shaking. His main problem became controlling his body's need to repeat certain movements, like drinking water from every fountain he passed. As his grades remained high and he felt less stress about schoolwork, Raymond realized he had a shot at a good college to train as an engineer.

Picture someone walking calmly down the hall and suddenly breaking into a hop-skip, arms punching the air. People stare. Others

High, who figured out how to use data from multiple observatories to quickly and accurately determine the distance of near-Earth asteroids.

However much raw ability they exhibit, many First Teamers credit their family environment. Beyond the classroom, many First Team members say they were exposed to a range of ideas and activities at an early age before finding the things that clicked with them. Some say visits to libraries and museums and family travels expanded their horizons. Others found their talents and interests piqued through music lessons, sports programs and summer and after-school camps. That commitment to their children is common among First Teamers' parents.

Mark Schneider was diagnosed with a mild case of Tourette's syndrome when he was in elementary school and is still prone to blinking and involuntary finger-snapping. Even before his diagnosis, Mark worked on his fine motor skills with his mom, Sandy, who encouraged him to draw ninja turtles, write letters to his favorite baseball players and do sleight-of-hand magic tricks.

"I don't think we saw Tourette's as that much of a threat. We saw it as something we all had to deal with. It's a part of who I am," says Mark, a senior at South Windsor (Conn.) High. Mark went on to create artwork displayed at the U.S. Capitol and to co-develop a computer model of West Nile virus transmission with his younger brother that won the $100,000 team prize at the Siemens Westinghouse Competition.

Mark also draws inspiration from his father. Ray Schneider was only a toddler when his own father died, but Ray ended up winning a scholarship to New York University and becoming an engineer. "Starting out with not a dime to his name, he has gone on to live a middle-class life with a two-car garage," Mark says.

—*Tracey Wong Briggs*

quickly move away or yell names. Now imagine another person watching a movie in a quiet theater. Suddenly, he or she has to let out loud grunts, curses, or racial slurs. They pierce the silence. Other viewers shout insults or yell at the person to be quiet.

How should people with these tics react, knowing they cannot prevent what their body does? Should they fight back? Should they refuse to go out in public? Or could they learn to live with the changing mix of uncontrollable behaviors that comes with Tourette syndrome?

These situations and more are what many people who have TS face every day. They frequently feel the need to explain that they're not crazy and not acting unusual on purpose—that they just have a neurological disorder that causes those actions.

FEELING BETTER ABOUT YOURSELF

Self-esteem can take a beating when TS accompanies the normal pressures of growing up. Extra criticism, teasing, and punishment add to the embarrassment and frustration of TS-related symptoms. But having TS should not prevent anyone from experiencing the world. Activities may take extra time and planning, and there will be disappointments along with the successes. But successes will happen. Once people accept their TS, they will feel more comfortable with themselves. Then they are ready to make friends, play instruments, join sports teams, date, work, drive, and do everything else other kids their age do.

"In order to live with Tourette syndrome, I think we must all learn to live—period," writes William Rubin, a psychologist and researcher who has TS. "That is, we must focus on things we would do if we did not have TS, and figure out ways to accomplish those things." While someone with TS can't ignore the problems it creates for them, Rubin says, "the more we can try to live our lives as others do, the better able we will be to handle the special burdens placed on us by the symptoms of TS."

BUILDING ON STRENGTHS

Anything that builds on interests, hobbies, and talents is more likely than not to bring success. And nothing develops self-esteem better than success. So taking part in activities based on interests can have great benefits for kids with TS.

For example, teens who like to write might join the school newspaper or yearbook staff, or they may keep a journal. Those

Keeping a journal can help teenagers with Tourette syndrome deal with the stress that often goes along with their condition.

who love sports might sign up for a school or community team sport. If team sports pose problems, sports lovers might consider noncontact sports, such as jogging, swimming, or tai chi. Animal lovers might buy a pet, offer to dog-sit for a neighbor, or seek a job at the local pet store. Each small success raises self-esteem another notch.

TAKING CONTROL OF LIFE

Gaining independence is another way to build self-esteem. Individuals who do things on their own feel better about themselves. Too often, however, families and schools use TS as an excuse. Parents and teachers never push a child to excel, or the child refuses to try. People assume that TS prevents someone from taking part in activities, so they never ask the person to join. These people believe they are helping, but they are actually sending the message that someone with TS is less capable, which isn't true.

Raymond explains, "My parents would say, 'We understand you cannot do this because of your tics.' It would upset me because I actually could do it, and they didn't give me the chance." He felt he could accomplish things if just given a little more time.

Children with TS cannot predict how others may react to them, but they can control the situations they are in and their own responses. This means taking responsibility for their actions. Responsibility involves speaking up to change situations at home, school, and on the job to adjust for TS-related symptoms.

Mark, who grew up with TS, stresses that point to others. "In TS camp, I teach that if you have motor tics, you may knock over a glass of water. I know you couldn't help it, but you should clean it up. You shouldn't have been that close. Similarly, if you have loud vocal tics, you should not be in a quiet room at the library. That's not being courteous, again, even though you cannot help it."

TO TELL OR NOT TO TELL

Many TS-related symptoms are invisible. Other people cannot read minds to understand why someone who tics says or does certain things. Therefore, communication becomes key to making life with TS easier. Yet whether or not to tell others about having TS is a personal choice. Often the decision boils down to comfort level—with themselves and with their condition—and age. The older people are, the more open they seem about explaining to new people about their TS.

"Tell them the truth," Jake suggests, though he admits that when he was younger, "I wouldn't tell anyone. I'd just say leave me alone.

It depends upon your personality if you tell people."

"Only this year did I start to tell people, my really good friends," sixteen-year-old Caroline adds.

Brian recalls, "When I was younger, [explaining TS] brought questions that I really didn't know how to answer at the time. Now if I know somebody will be in my life a long time, I tell them about TS. But I don't need to tell acquaintances when it doesn't come up—not that I'm ashamed of it."

HOW OTHERS CAN HELP SOMEONE WHO TICS

For many people with TS, social situations worsen their tics. They sense that friends, classmates, and family are watching and listening for symptoms. They feel uncomfortable with bullies who cannot understand them and with strangers who don't know about Tourette syndrome. They want classmates and coworkers to know there is a real person beyond the movements and sounds. Caroline, Raymond, and Mark suggested how others can help someone with TS feel more comfortable:

"Don't tell jokes about it," Caroline advises. "Just act as if I wasn't doing anything. Somebody once was mean. It felt like a punch in the stomach."

"Support me and don't bring it up," Raymond recommends. "I like talking about it sometimes, but others should make sure they don't offend me by saying anything."

"If someone tells you they have TS, believe them. Don't mimic them," Mark urges. "Don't ask them to repeat their tics because if they weren't ticcing, asking will set them off. Don't accuse them of being able to control tics. Don't try to be funny and respond to their coprolalia with a joke. Just try to be understanding that they cannot help it."

HELPING YOURSELF

SUBSTITUTING ONE ACTION FOR ANOTHER

Some people find they can replace tics with more socially acceptable movements and still satisfy the original urge. They perform a movement similar to the original tic. Substitutions help relieve tics that cause pain or danger, such as lip biting, head jerking, or wrist banging.

"I had this big sore in my mouth from biting," Caroline remembers. "I would scrape under it to relieve the urge [to bite it], so it wouldn't hurt so much and it wouldn't be so noticeable."

"I mask putting my finger up my nose by blowing my nose," Mark explains. "And I try to cover up a grunt with a cough. I can also focus on somebody or something really intensely so I won't tic. I just have to find something to talk about and get going."

LEARNING TO RELAX

Studies show that when someone with Tourette syndrome relaxes, so do their tics. But most children and adults—with and without TS—lead very scheduled, stress-filled lives. Therefore, it's important to carve out time to kick back and renew energy, which contributes to positive mental health.

Meditation. Some people believe meditation helps them tic less. This method of relaxing requires focusing on a single word or object. Once the mind refocuses, it draws attention away from distracting thoughts that may cause stress. As stress leaves the mind, blood pressure goes down and muscle tension eases.

Exercise. Exercise is the best natural tranquilizer. Any form of exercise will give benefits, whether it's walking, running, biking, swimming, dancing, or playing sports. Regular physical activity sparks production of brain chemicals that relieve depression and pent-up tension caused by the urge to tic. Exercise also burns more

Getting regular exercise not only helps keep the body healthy but also can produce chemicals in the brain that relieve depression and tension in people with TS.

calories as the body works faster, which helps control weight gain from medication. In addition, people feel calmer after exercise. For many people with TS, exercise reduces the frequency and force of their tics and eases the pain from muscles tightened due to repeated movements. Exercise can also lessen symptoms of ADHD and OCD. Exercisers generally feel better both in body and in mind.

Raymond agrees. "When I'm doing a sport, I tic a lot less because I'm not paying attention to everything. I'm thinking about the sport, like kicking the ball in soccer."

Relaxing to music. For individuals who have trouble staying still, music gives them purpose. Peaceful sounds, such as ocean waves

Life
SECTION D
LIFE.USATODAY.COM

April 26, 2010

From the Pages of USA TODAY

Exercise vs. anxiety

Most people seeking treatment for depression or anxiety face two choices: medication or psychotherapy. But there's a third choice that is rarely prescribed, though it comes with few side effects, low costs and a list of added benefits, advocates say. The treatment: exercise.

"It's become clear that this is a good intervention, particularly for mild to moderate depression," says Jasper Smits, a psychologist at Southern Methodist University in Dallas, Texas. Exercise as an anxiety treatment is less well-studied but looks helpful, he says.

It's no secret that exercise often boosts mood: the runner's high is legendary, and walkers, bikers, dancers and swimmers report their share of bliss. Now data pooled from many small studies suggest that in people diagnosed with depression or anxiety, the immediate mood boost is followed by longer-term relief, similar to that

or soothing music, focus the brain. When the brain is occupied, the body becomes calmer. Studies confirm that music slows breathing and blood flow and lowers muscle tension, which may reduce tics and help the body rest.

Visualization. Research supports a strong connection between body and mind. Many people find that closing their eyes and creating a mental picture of health frees them of stress. They imagine the picture as detailed and real as possible. For example, people with wild arm and leg tics may envision their body lying still, with just one body part at a time gently moving. The idea behind visualization is for the mind to send the body a message that it is strong and can heal itself.

offered by medication and talk therapy, says Daniel Landers, professor emeritus of kinesiology at Arizona State University. And exercise seems to work better than relaxation, meditation, stress education and music therapy, Landers says.

Ideally, Smits says, depressed or anxious people would get written exercise prescriptions, complete with suggested "doses" and strategies for getting started and sticking with the program. One thing that helps people keep up this therapy, he says, is the immediate boost that many report. The same can't be said of taking pills.

But Smits and other exercise-as-treatment enthusiasts are quick to say that medication and psychotherapy are good treatments, too, and can be combined with exercise.

What kinds of exercise works? Most studies have focused on aerobic exercise, such as running and walking, but had not ruled out strength training or other regimens.

How much is needed? At least one study shows results from the amount recommended for physical health: 150 minutes of moderate exercise (such as brisk walking) or 75 minutes of vigorous exercise (such as running) each week.

How does it help? Does it boost certain brain chemicals? Induce deeper sleep? Give patients a sense of action and accomplishment? Can it prevent depression and anxiety?

That seems likely, says Michelle Riba, a psychiatrist at the University of Michigan. "I don't think exercise will ever be the only treatment, but it may be a major part of preventing recurrences. It should be part of everybody's plan of health."

—Kim Painter

Yoga and tai chi. Two forms of movement, yoga and tai chi, emphasize the mind-body connection. The ancient Hindu system of yoga combines deep breathing with physical poses that slowly stretch muscles through a series of movements. Over time, yoga can produce greater muscle strength and flexibility. The Chinese system of tai chi uses movement to increase body awareness and control. Each of the more than one hundred movements begins with the body in a different position. Constant slow movements result in inner stillness. Tai chi fans believe that these poses create a perfect union of body and mind. Although neither approach has been proven to affect tics, both are known to improve body tone and overall health and well-being.

FIGHTING DISCRIMINATION

Several laws protect the rights of people with disabilities. The laws guarantee access to education, jobs, public places, transportation, and government services. Even with these laws, discrimination happens. Kids with TS get suspended from school for hyperactivity, raging, or coprolalia. Adults who tic have difficulty finding and keeping jobs.

Several individuals have filed lawsuits against organizations, such as airlines or housing developments, for refusing people with TS. In one case, Eric Thompson was denied a job after performing well in the company's training program. The company paid him a large sum to settle the lawsuit he filed. But Eric was even more pleased by the publicity his case got. "A lot of people learned about Tourette syndrome. I've never had any trouble working because of my condition; I didn't consider it a legal handicap. I knew what I could do. People with [TS] need to stand up for themselves."

Individuals with TS who feel their rights have been violated can contact the Tourette Syndrome Association, their local government department of disabilities or fair employment, or the Family Resource Center on Disabilities, which coordinates information centers nationwide (see Resources). These groups know the laws and how to help people with disabilities receive the fair treatment they deserve.

KEEPING A SENSE OF HUMOR

Tics can look goofy. They can erupt at the most inconvenient times. Being able to laugh at oneself about these situations relieves tension. Yes, tics are awful at times. But they cannot change the person inside. Tics are only one part of who someone is. Laughter helps keep TS in perspective.

"If I can get my sense of humor to take over [when tics are embarrassing], that usually helps," Mark notes. "Even though I have a warped sense of humor, it usually makes people laugh."

THINKING POSITIVELY ABOUT THE FUTURE

Kids with TS tally a rich list of achievements. Raymond excels in math and will enter a university program to be an engineer. Jake plays soccer. Brian has a flair for creative writing and acting. Caroline gets good grades and enjoys cooking. Every day these people prove they are more than their tics.

A small percentage of adults continue to struggle with life-altering tics. These individuals enter every walk of life. They become teachers, lawyers, scientists, secretaries, mechanics, doctors, and salespeople. Some say TS boosts their careers. Big-name athletes claim they benefit from the quick, coordinated movements that come with TS. Artists insist that the wildness of their tics inspires rushes of creativity for colorful visions, musical themes, and fantastic story lines. All try to make the most of their talents.

As Brian reasons, "I am proud of who I am. I might change in five or six years. My whole life story isn't written out yet."

GLOSSARY

antibodies: substances created in the body to fight off disease

autoimmune reaction: a situation when substances in the body that are supposed to fight infection attack healthy tissue as well

basal ganglia: nerve clusters deep within the brain that play a role in smooth muscle actions and stopping and starting movement. The basal ganglia is thought to be the area of the brain involved with tics.

biofeedback: a procedure that retrains the brain through exercises that monitor brain responses by computer

caudate nucleus: an area within the basal ganglia portion of the brain that transmits messages from the brain to control movement

central adrenergic inhibitors: a class of medications that help control behavior symptoms of TS

cerebrum: the largest portion of the brain. Most conscious and intelligence activity occurs here. The cerebrum is the site of language, sensation, voluntary movement, memory, emotion, and imagination.

cognitive behavior therapy: organized treatment with a therapist that retrains the brain to react differently in trouble-producing situations, reducing compulsions

complex tics: coordinated patterns of movements involving several muscle groups

compulsions: actions someone must perform to ease discomfort caused by certain repeated distressful thoughts or images

coprolalia: a complex vocal tic that involves cursing or saying socially inappropriate words

copropraxia: a complex motor tic that involves making offensive gestures

dopamine: a neurotransmitter that regulates movement and balance. Excess dopamine triggers severe tics.

echolalia: a complex vocal tic that involves repeating the last sound, word, or phrase said by someone else

echopraxia: a complex motor tic that involves imitating someone else's actions

genes: basic units of heredity present on a chromosome. Genes determine physical and other traits and are passed from parents to child.

Human Genome Project: a national research program that sought to provide a map of the genes that make up human DNA

Individuals with Disabilities Education Act (IDEA): a federal law dating to 1990 that requires schools to provide education to any student with a disability in the least restrictive environment

mecamylamine: a nicotine-like drug for high blood pressure that is being tested for use to reduce tics

motor tics: sudden uncontrollable movements that arise from muscles of the body

neuroleptics: a common class of medications prescribed for tics that suppresses the action of dopamine, the chemical that transmits impulses between nerve cells

neurologist: a medical doctor who specializes in the nervous system

neurotransmitter: a chemical in the brain that carries messages from one brain cell to another

nicotine: the drug in tobacco that makes smoking addictive but that can increase the manufacture of dopamine in the brain enough to shut down its production and reduce tics

norepinephrine: a neurotransmitter that may influence how messages in the brain control movement

obsessions: thoughts or images that return over and over again, interfering with everyday activities

palilalia: a complex vocal tic that involves repeating one's own words or sounds

pediatrician: a medical doctor who specializes in caring for children and adolescents

psychiatrist: a medical doctor who specializes in mental problems and who can prescribe medication

psychologist: someone who is trained to counsel patients with emotional or behavior problems but cannot prescribe medication

psychotherapy: treatment of mental and behavioral disorders using verbal and nonverbal communication without physical intervention

resource room: a room within a school in which small numbers of students receive extra attention so they can handle their schoolwork in a regular class setting

serotonin: a neurotransmitter that affects emotion, balance, and thought and that transmits messages from the brain involving movement

simple tics: individual repeated movements of only one body part, such as head jerking

special needs class: a separate full-time classroom for students with disabilities who need adapted learning situations

stimulant: a type of medication given to treat conditions such as ADHD. Stimulants boost the flow of brain chemicals involved in increasing attention and concentration.

streptococcus: a bacteria that invades the body and could play a role in triggering tics. Streptococcus is called strep for short.

syndrome: a collection of observed symptoms, with no medical tests to prove its existence

tardive dyskinesia: a movement disorder that sometimes results from taking neuroleptics

testosterone: the primary male sex hormone

tics: movements and sounds beyond a person's control

tranquilizer: a type of medication that helps regulate neurotransmitters in the brain

vocal tics: sudden uncontrollable sounds that come from muscles controlling speech

RESOURCES

These organizations provide additional information about Tourette syndrome and related conditions. An Internet search can help you find government agencies that may change locations with administrations.

Association of University Centers on Disabilities Programs for Persons with Developmental Disabilities
1010 Wayne Avenue, Suite 920
Silver Spring, MD 20910
(301) 588-8252
http://www.aucd.org
This network of centers works toward improving policies and practices involving people with disabilities, their families, and the community.

CHADD (Children and Adults with Attention Deficit/Hyperactivity Disorder)
8181 Professional Place, Suite 150
Landover, MD 20785
(800) 233-4050
http://www.chadd.org
Visit CHADD's rich website for information about ADHD in children and adults, support through local groups or online, professional referrals, and conferences concerning ADHD.

Family Resource Center on Disabilities
20 East Jackson Boulevard, Room 300
Chicago, IL 60604
9312) 939-3513
http://www.frcd.org
This nonprofit agency provides information, referrals, and advocacy tips for families of children with disabilities.

International OCD Foundation (IOCDF)
PO Box 961029
Boston, MA 02196
(617) 973-5801
http://ocfoundation.org
The IOCDF provides a wealth of information, as well as professional referrals, local groups, and conferences concerning obsessive-compulsive disorder.

Learning Disabilities Association of America (LDA)
4156 Library Road
Pittsburgh, PA 15234-1349
(412) 341-1515
http://www.ldanatl.org
This national organization provides information on learning disabilities for parents, teachers, professionals, and others. Visit this website for state chapters, updates on relevant laws, and upcoming conferences.

National Dissemination Center for Children with Disabilities
1825 Connecticut Avenue NW
Suite 700
Washington, DC 20009
(800) 695-0285
http://www.nichcy.org
Visit the website of this public agency for information on disabilities in children of different ages, IDEA and education laws, and Spanish-language informational pages.

National Human Genome Research Institute
National Institutes of Health
Building 31, Room 4B09
31 Center Drive, MSC 2152
9000 Rockville Pike
Bethesda, MD 20892-2152
(301) 402-0911
http://www.genome.gov
The genetic research arm of the National Institutes of Health supports research and distributes up-to-date information about causes and the treatment of many child development issues, including Tourette syndrome. This website features the most recent results of genetic research.

National Institute of Neurological Disorders and Stroke (NINDS)
Silver Spring, MD 20824
(800) 352-9424 or (301) 496-5751
http://www.ninds.nih.gov
This branch of the National Institutes of Health provides information about neurological problems and research programs.

National Organization for Rare Disorders (NORD)
55 Kenosia Avenue
PO Box 1968
New Fairfield, CT 06813
(800) 999-6673
http://www.rarediseases.org
This organization provides free and fee-based information about rare diseases, including Tourette syndrome; a medication assistance program for families who cannot afford drugs; and diagnostic and treatment referrals.

Tourette Syndrome Association, Inc. (TSA)
42-40 Bell Blvd., Suite 205
Bayside, New York 11361-2820
(718) 224-2999
http://www.tsa-usa.org
This national organization for Tourette syndrome provides referrals to local TSA chapters, physicians, and advocacy resources. TSA offers print and video information and workshops about all aspects of Tourette syndrome, including two newsletters for readers of different ages. Local chapters run support groups and camps for families touched by TS. The organization also offers several downloadable publications written by members.

SOURCE NOTES

5   Caroline, personal interview with author, Wilmette, IL, August 10, 2000.

12 Jason Valencia, *Tourette's Syndrome: A Young Man's Poetic Journey through Childhood* (Skokie, IL: Tourette Syndrome Association, 1998), 2.

21 Oliver Sacks, *An Anthropologist on Mars* (New York: Knopf, 1995), 97.

22 Mark, personal interview with author, Lincolnwood, IL, January 14, 2001.

24 Aaron's mother, personal interview with author, San Diego, CA, October 4, 2000.

26 Mark, personal interview.

28 Aaron, personal interview with author, San Diego, CA, October 4, 2000.

28–29 Jake, personal interview with author, Northbrook, IL, October 16, 2000.

31 Brian, personal interview with author, Chicago, IL, September 24, 2000.

32–33 Howard Kushner, *A Cursing Brain?: The Histories of Tourette Syndrome*, (Cambridge, MA: Harvard University Press, 1999), 11.

46 Jake, personal interview.

50 Mark, personal interview.

52 Adam's mother, personal interview with author, Wilmette, IL, January 20, 2001.

56 Brian, personal interview.

57 Raymond's mother, personal interview with author, Glencoe, IL, November 2, 2000.

59 Caroline's mother, personal interview with author, Wilmette, IL, August 10, 2001.

62 Raymond, personal interview with author, Glencoe, IL, November 2, 2000.

67 Aaron's mother, personal interview.

68 Ibid.

69 Ibid.

70 Elaine Shimberg, *Living with Tourette Syndrome* (New York: Simon & Schuster, 1995), 123.

70 Brian, personal interview.

71 Tourette Syndrome Association, "TS in the Family: Brother and Sisters Coping Together," *Tourette Syndrome Association Newsletter*, 28, no. 3 (Winter 2000): 1.

72 Ibid.

72 Jake's mother, personal interview, Northbrook, IL, October 16, 2000.

74 Ibid.

77 Adam's mother, personal interview.

78 Raymond's mother, personal interview.

84 Raymond, personal interview.

88 William Rubin, "Living with Tourette Syndrome: 'I Am Not My Tics!'" in Tracy Lynne Marsh, ed., *Children with Tourette Syndrome: A Parents' Guide* (Rockville, MD: Woodbine House, 2007), 298.

90 Raymond, personal interview.

90 Mark, personal interview.

90–91 Jake, personal interview.

91 Caroline, personal interview.

91 Brian, personal interview.

91 Caroline, personal interview.

91 Raymond, personal interview.

91 Mark, personal interview.

92 Caroline, personal interview.

92 Mark, personal interview.

93 Raymond, personal interview.

96 "Tracing Workplace Problems to Hidden Disorders: Tourette Syndrome," *Personnel Journal*, 71, no. 6 (June 1992): 92–93.

97 Mark, personal interview.

97 Brian, personal interview.

SELECTED BIBLIOGRAPHY

Friesen, Jonathan. *Jerk, California*. New York: Speak, 2008.

Handler, Lowell. *Twitch and Shout: A Touretter's Tale*. Minneapolis: University of Minnesota Press, 2004.

Kushner, Howard. *A Cursing Brain?: The Histories of Tourette Syndrome*. Cambridge, MA: Harvard University Press, 1999.

Patterson, James, and Hal Friedman. *Against Medical Advice: A True Story*. New York: Little, Brown and Co., 2008.

Wilensky, Amy. *Passing for Normal: A Memoir of Compulsion*. New York: Broadway Books, 1999.

FURTHER READING AND WEBSITES

Books

For Students:

Buffolano, Sandra. *Coping with Tourette Syndrome: A Workbook for Kids with Tic Disorders*. Oakland: Instant Help Books, 2008.

Hyde, Margaret O., and Elizabeth H. Forsyth, M.D. *Stress 101: An Overview for Teens*. Minneapolis: Twenty-First Century Books, 2008.

Moe, Barbara. *Coping with Tourette Syndrome and Tic Disorders*. New York: Rosen Publishing Group, 2000.

For Brothers and Sisters:

Meyer, Donald. *The Sibling*. Bethesda, MD: Woodbine, 2005.

——. *Slam Books: What It's Really Like for a Brother or Sister with Special Needs*. Bethesda, MD: Woodbine, 2005.

Strohm. Kate. *Being the Other One*. Boston: Shambhala, 2005.

For Parents, Teachers, and Older Readers:

Cohen, Brad. *Front of the Class: How Tourette Syndrome Made Me the Teacher I Never Had*. New York: St. Martin's Griffin, 2008.

Hughes, Susan. *What Makes Ryan Tick?* Toronto: Hope Press, 2003.

Maloney, Beth Alison. *Serving Sammy: Curing the Boy Who Caught OCD*. New York: Crown, 2009.

Sacks, Oliver. *The Man Who Mistook His Wife for a Hat and Other Clinical Tales*. New York: Touchstone, 1998.

Seligman, Adam. *Don't Think about Monkeys*. Toronto: Hope Press, 1992.

Websites

National Institute of Mental Health
http://www.nimh.nih.gov

Visit this government source for studies related to TS and information on a wide variety of mental health issues.

National Institutes of Health
http://www.ninds.nih.gov/disorders/tourette/detail_tourette.htm

This page from the National Institutes of Health answers many frequently asked questions about TS.

Tourette Syndrome
http://kidshealth.org/kid/health_problems/brain/k_tourette.html

KidsHealth has several online pages explaining TS and related conditions to kids, teens, and parents.

Tourette Syndrome "Plus"
http://www.tourettesyndrome.net

This site includes a wealth of articles on TS and associated disorders, including recent research and tips for school and behavioral issues.

LERNER
SOURCE™

Expand learning beyond the printed book. Download free, complementary educational resources for this book from our website, www.lerneresource.com.

INDEX

ABOUT THE AUTHOR

Marlene Targ Brill is an award-winning author of sixty seven books for readers of all ages. She writes about many different topics, but as a former special educator, she particularly enjoys writing about people with special needs. Her goal in writing books like *Tourette Syndrome* is to help communities better understand these medical issues, so people who have them are treated equally and without discrimination.

PHOTO ACKNOWLEDGMENTS

The images in this book are used with the permission of: © Bjorn Meyer/The Agency Collection/Getty Images, pp. 1, 3; © Doctor Stock/Science Faction/CORBIS, p. 4; © Robert Hanashiro/USA TODAY, pp. 7, 61; © Gail Oskin/Stringer/Getty Images, p. 9; © Digital Vision/Getty Images, p. 10; © Christopher Gannon/USA TODAY, p. 19; © Tom Dillon/USA TODAY, p. 20; © Katye Martens/USA TODAY, p. 24; © Jose Luis Pelaez Inc./Blend Images/Getty Images, p. 27; © Kritina Lee Knief/Photographer's Choice/Getty Images, p. 29; © Tanya Constantine/Photodisc/Getty Images, p. 30; Courtesy of the National Library of Medicine, p. 32; Wellcome Library, London, p. 34; © Dan MacMedan/USA TODAY, p. 37; © Laura Westlund/Independent Picture Service, pp . 38, 39, 41 © age fotostock/SuperStock, p. 44; © Stock Connection/ SuperStock, p. 46; © SW Productions/Photodisc/Getty Images, p. 49; © Doug Martin/Photo Researchers, Inc., p. 52; © Todd Strand/Independent Picture Service, p. 57; © Mark Peterson/CORBIS, p. 59; © Tetra Images/Getty Images, p. 64; © Stefanie Grewel/CORBIS, p. 67; © Blend Images/the Agency Collection/Getty Images, p. 68; © Purestock/Getty Images, p. 73; © Fuse/Getty Images, p. 79; © Thomas Barwick/Taxi/Getty Images, p. 82; © Moment/Cultura/Getty Images, p. 85; © Jamie Grill/Iconica/Getty Images, p. 89; © Jupiterimages/Comstock Images/ Getty Images, p. 93.

Front Cover: © Bjorn Meyer/The Agency Collection/Getty Images.

Main body text set in USA TODAY Roman 10/15.